MECANOO
Inspiration and Process in Architecture

Edited by
Francesca Serrazanetti, Matteo Schubert

Published by Moleskine Srl

Series and Book Editors
Francesca Serrazanetti, Matteo Schubert

Publishing Director
Roberto Di Puma

Graphic design
A+G AchilliGhizzardiAssociati

ISBN 978-88-6613-165-6

No part of this book may be reproduced
in any form without written permission from
the copyrights owners and the publisher.

© 2017 Moleskine Srl
© 2017 Mecanoo for the images
© 2017 Francesca Serrazanetti, Matteo Schubert
© All rights reserved

Text by Francesca Serrazanetti
and Matteo Schubert

Moleskine© is a registered trademark

First edition October 2017
Printed in Italy by Galli Thierry

We would like to thank
Rogier Coopmans and Eliano Felicio, Mecanoo

Inspiration and Process in Architecture is a series of monographs on key figures in modern and contemporary architecture. It offers a reading of the practice of design which emphasises the value of freehand drawing as part of the creative process. Each volume provides a different perspective, revealing secrets and insights and showing the various observation techniques languages, characters, forms and means of communication.

Contents

5 Writings
6 Plunging headfirst into Mecanoo's creative process
9 Interview with Francine Houben

21 Drawings
22 Visualizing
68 Recording
82 Diagramming
100 Assembling
118 Modelling

139 Biography

"Architecture must appeal to all the senses.
Architecture is never a purely intellectual,
conceptual, or visual game alone. Architecture is
about combining all the individual elements into
a single concept. What counts in the end
is the arrangement of form and emotion."
Sketch by Francine Houben

Writings

Plunging headfirst into Mecanoo's creative process

Headed by Francine Houben, who trained at Delft University of Technology, the Dutch practice Mecanoo applies three fundamental concepts to every architectural scale and project without exception: designing for people; paying close attention to the place where the architecture is shaped; and defining the purpose of the project in a precise and relevant way. In all the office's work you can retrace the constant research and inspiration embodied in the details tailored to the places where their buildings are set. This analysis results in actions that create ever different solutions without replicating or reiterating the projects it has already built. Mecanoo skillfully combines the disciplines of architecture, urban planning and landscape in non-traditional ways, with deep sensitivity and a particular concern for light and nature. This approach reveals the practice's roots deeply embedded in the culture of the Netherlands, a "land of water, wind and clouds," where Mecanoo is based and has its origins: in a landscape that is never static, one that over the centuries has been subjected to constant, far-reaching changes. The work of Francine Houben and her team also lays great stress on beauty and aesthetic qualities, heightening them through a compelling yet playful use of innovative materials and designs. All their projects use colors, textures and materials adroitly, creating richly contrasting compositions.

The figure of the diver adopted by the group comes from a wooden stamp picked up in a flea market. It is an icon of clear thinking: the courage and freedom to plunge into the void, experimenting with new architectural languages and exploring new regions. This interest in innovation is evident in the practice's creative processes and its projects: it keeps a firm grip on reality and devotes constant attention to the settings in which it works. It signals an open-ended approach, one that can be altered and adapted by experimenting with new compositional practices and assembling heterogeneous elements.

In 2000 Francine Houben devised a sort of manifesto setting out the ten principles guiding the office's work: "land as expensive commodity," which we have to respect and care for; "love of nature" and the materials that compose it; "collective responsibility for sustainability," namely water management as a condition of survival; "wealth of urban planning," responding to the transformations of contemporary living; "cooperation as challenge," networking different professions into a collective rationale; "director and script writer," or the architect's new role in relation to the client; "handwriting and language," with the use of different idioms and going beyond the concept of style; "composition of empty space," as an essential part of architecture; "analysis and intuition," a combination of curiosity, concern and experiment essential to the project; "arrangement of form and emotion," which has to guide the project as well as the perception of architecture using all the senses.

A multidisciplinary approach and a broader outlook thus supersede the concept of style, going beyond the attempt to establish an unambiguous, unique language. Architecture has to be able to speak different languages, relate to different places and interlocutors, change and hybridize an assortment of expressions and disciplines.

With the same curiosity and freedom as the diver in the Mecanoo logo, this book tries to shed light on the different phases of the work process by bringing together projects built at different times. The aim is to correlate techniques, instruments and project forms that have certainly evolved over the years but have also characterized the practice throughout its history. Analyzing the great body of work produced in the project phase from 1984 to the present brings out certain common matrices, which identify different practices in its design work. For this reason the illustrations in the volume are organized into sections that identify certain design instruments. *Visualization* takes the prevalent form of representations made by hand, whether they are sketches, exploded views, axonometric projections, sections, or perspectives. The ability to *record* and enhance some of the precise dimensions present on the scene of the project makes use of sketches and photographs; their translation into *diagrams* is useful for defining the flows and functioning of the architectural machine and transposing these data into the composition; artistic *assemblies* of photos, images and drawings made by hand or computer represent the image and sometimes also the metaphorical value of architecture; last but not least, the *models*, which have always accompanied the studio's work, allow for verification, direct contact and a plunge into the design in a way no digital technique can offer.

As Francine Houben says, the architect does not work alone on the project. The architect is now a stage director, working with a hybrid and complex screenplay. The architect is the figure who, understanding the client's wishes, creates the story and builds the context through ideas, images, atmospheres, scale models and drawings. The instruments used by the stage director are recounted and brought together in this volume. While each chapter corresponds to a specific phase of the process, careful analysis can decipher the coordinates underlying all the projects in quest of "beauty," which, as Houben says, is a combination of introverted and extroverted, heavy and light, tactile and abstract: a screenplay written by multiple hands to respond in the best possible way to every new challenge.

Interview with Francine Houben

❝ *Your office has crossed the historical divide from manual to digital design. What has it lost or gained?*

At Mecanoo we've always tried to balance manual and digital. In our early days, we were quick to adopt digital technologies because we wanted to be up to date with all the new tools. These days we're very advanced with 3D printing and virtual and augmented reality. On the other hand, we still keep doing sketches and making models. We have our model making shop in house. The tools we use for projects depend on who the client is and what the audience is. It also depends on who's in the team. Some people are good at model making, whereas others can't even do a sketch but have excellent skills in 3D. What we do is a kind of remixing with skills.

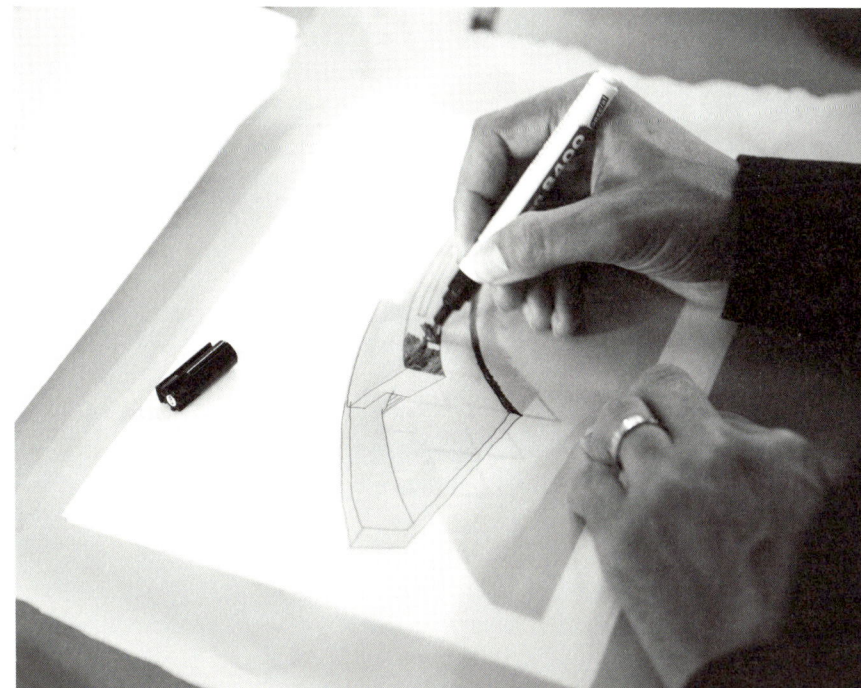

❝ *How do you combine creative and functional requirements in your design work?*

First of all, architects always have to deal with functional things. Architecture is not an autonomous art form. Secondly, creative and functional requirements aren't in opposition to each other. They are part of the same thing and the essence of architectural design is to have a good vision of how to handle this combination skillfully.

❝ *Models seem to be a much-used tool in your practice, both in the concept phase and in the final presentation of the project. What does this tool offer compared to 3D computer views?*

Models and 3D computer views cannot be compared. They really exist beside one another, catering to different senses both in the design process and the presentation to clients and users. 3D imagery is highly visual and immersive, models are tactile and spatial. CGI images and virtual reality are often individual experiences, whereas you can look at a model together, walk around it and even touch it.

❝ *Your designs and concepts often take the forms of diagrams or schemes. Can you explain the reason for this and its value?*

If you have a certain concept, a diagram can be an important way to illustrate your idea. Concepts should be readable in more ways than one. A good building is never based on just one idea, it's always based on multiple ideas. This also makes the concept stronger for the future, and more capable of appealing to everyone's expectations.

To me, functional diagrams are also a way of trying to understand the material in hand, what I call "The Clay". What is in your fingers? How can you sculpt it? If you don't do that analysis, you will not have an idea of how to design a building. You need a kind of feeling of

11

the composition, and to understand how big or small things are and how they relate. In order to play with "The Clay", you really need to know it.

❝ *The theme of color seems to play a significant part in both your drawings and projects. Why?*

Color is very important. When I first started working for an avant-garde theater group in 1995 I came to understand the value of color. I went to a lot of performances and the directors showed me how to play with light and colors.
In a way, colors became like a material to me and you can see that in many of our designs: Mecanoo blue, a special dark red or gold and silver are used often. The green of grass can be considered a material as well.

I always make this joke that I don't want green things inside, because green is what you see when you look out of the window, it's nature. In compositions of materials, colors and light, the green is outside.

❝ *Some of your works are frequently presented and associated with architectural references, suggestions or memories that have guided the initial idea. How do you register and organize these informational criteria?*

The different references which influence the designs are usually very personal. It can be a memory from my youth or an experience, or the way I observed a certain city or a certain country. Together, they amount to a kind of storytelling, a way to build up the concept. I don't collect the information by writing it down, but I mainly register it in photographs. I take a lot of photos. Not pretty pictures, but ones that explain a context or culture. To me, it's important to see things and observe.

For instance, I was born in the southeast of the Netherlands which has a gently sloping landscape with soft hills and solitary trees. The rest of the country is very flat. I often try to make little hills because I like the way they function in the sequence of moving through a space, or through the city or the landscape.

❝ *Each office goes through different phases and relies, in the course of its history, on designers or other key figures that affect their subsequent works. Could you mention some key encounters, even going back to your years at university?*

I met Charles and Ray Eames several times in the late 70s and early 80s. In 1985 I met Toyo Ito and Kazuyo Sejima during my trip to Japan. Meeting these Japanese architects who were not well-known at the time was very important.

Álvaro Siza worked from our office in the 1980s. We were the local architect for a project he designed in The Hague. To work with him was a real eye-opener for me.

At the Delft University of Technology, we were taught to approach everything very rationally. Siza's formal language and his way of sketching, encouraged me to take more freedom.

As a student I worked with Max Risselada. He was really influential in my teaching and it was him that put me in touch with the Eameses, because he used to work with them. Another inspirational collaboration was with Wubbo Ockels. He was the first astronaut in the Netherlands and he had a very innovative way of thinking about sustainability and looking to the future.

❝ *Your projects, mostly in recent years, seem to deviate from the "Dutch school," which was very influential in your early career, and offer more "international" and organic solutions. How did you develop this identity?*

When I started as an architect I was 25 years old. I was still a student at that time, and deeply influenced by what I was taught at the Delft University of Technology. We could play really well with floor plans and typologies, but to use materials in an expressive manner, you need more knowledge. To be a really good architect, you also need a lot of experience.

It took 15 to 20 years of thinking about materials and developing our identity. That's why it was important to work with Siza, who gave me much more freedom to think. Combining rationality and freedom, education and practice, is a great experience.

❝ *What interdisciplinary exchanges have influenced your work or individual projects in your multi-year history?*

They range from art to engineering: the two need each other. I've always been a great fan of David Hockney and his innovative attitude to photographing and filming. Moving through some of the villas that we designed, it almost feels like you're in the Jacques Tati movie "Les Vacances de Monsieur Hulot". And, as I mentioned before, in our work you can recognize the influence of theater directors. What was also very important to me was my own research into mobility, working together with a wide range of experts from all over the world. This cross-pollination of technical disciplines was something that I experienced strongly in Delft at the University of Technology.

❝ *Your design process seems to be open-ended, capable of being influenced and moved by external inputs. It's interesting, for example, to see how you worked together with the cartoonist Joost Swarte on the Toneelschuur Theater in Haarlem. His drawings interacted directly with the project development. How does this kind of relationship work?*

Our work doesn't have a single formal language. You can recognize Mecanoo's designs, but not because they are always white or always blue or always shaped the same form. We look at the setting to see what is needed. Working with Joost Swarte on the Toneelschuur Theater in Haarlem, he was officially the design director and we were the executive architects. This kind of relationship is an enriching experience, and it helps other people at the same time. As a cartoonist, Joost Swarte looks at materials in completely different way. With Siza it also worked both ways. We were his local architects and he created the design. You learn a lot by working together and not always being in the lead.

❝ *The relation with people is at the center of your idea of architecture. You think of architecture as a breathing and changing space, and your drawings are often inhabited with people. How do you develop the project by paying attention to the place and the people who live (or will live) in it?*

From the beginning, our work has been very human. My philosophy has recently been outlined in the book *People Place Purpose* (Artifice, 2015). When I did this book, I had been working as an architect for 30 years. What I learned in those 30 years is that the purpose always changes and places are always different. The one thing that doesn't change that much is people, people's senses and the proportions of people. And how space is shaped around people and their senses. Architecture must appeal to all the senses. Acoustics are extremely important, as well as how to deal with daylight and artificial light, or the tactility of materials.

And even what you don't see in pictures, like the natural ventilation system to get fresh air into a building, ensuring people feel comfortable in it.

To give an example, we've done a lot of urban planning. The materials I use in urban planning are often conceived for the development of young children. If you just make everything asphalt or concrete tiles, they don't develop their senses properly. So it's vital to enrich their potential in parks, in streets, in a neighborhood or by making some of those little hills. A variety of trees can show how the seasons change, the same goes for flowers. People say you develop your senses when you're a child. It's extremely important for the younger generations that we stimulate their senses through architecture and urban design.

Kaohsiung Public Library
Kaohsiung, 2011

Drawings

Visualizing

In more than thirty years' work, Mecanoo has experienced and traversed all the stages of innovation and changes in representation caused by the ascent of computers. As you look at the different materials published in the following pages, it is worth observing the unflagging use of traditional techniques of representation, using instruments such as pencils, pens, colored crayon or watercolors. Textures, colors, surfaces and compositional principles are given material form on paper, thanks to immediate and effective visualization. In recent years, amid the endless sketches and freehand notes, there have emerged bird's eye views, perspectives or hybrid axonometric projections, where the use of the computer has made it possible to generate highly effective images without losing the poetry and tactility of the manual gesture. Another interesting point is the plurality of traits and languages typical of a team in which different people and sensibilities act on the same project, enriching it with their gazes.

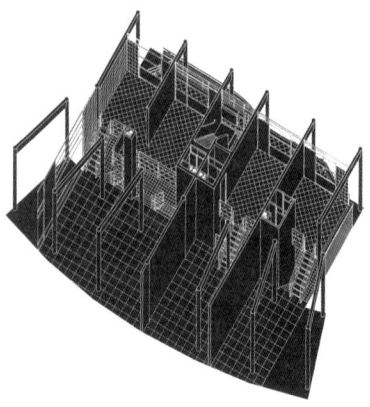 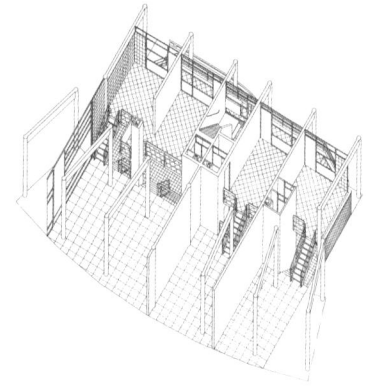

left and right
Kruisplein
Rotterdam, 1983

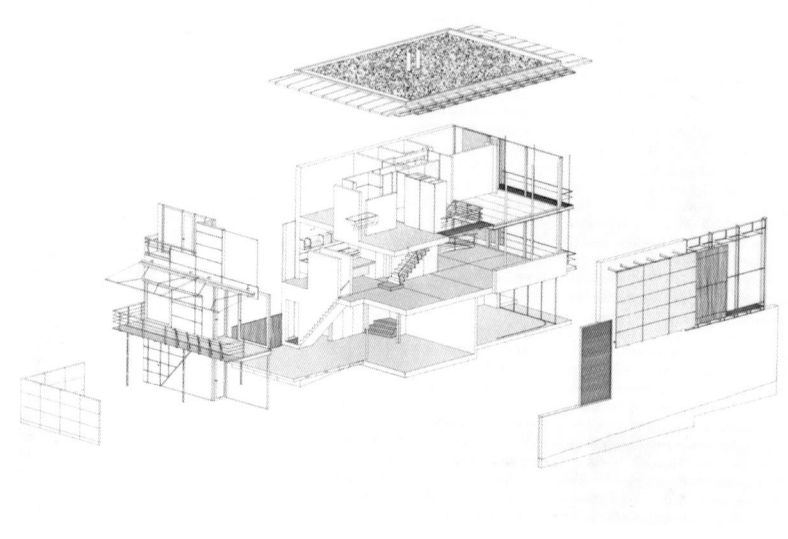
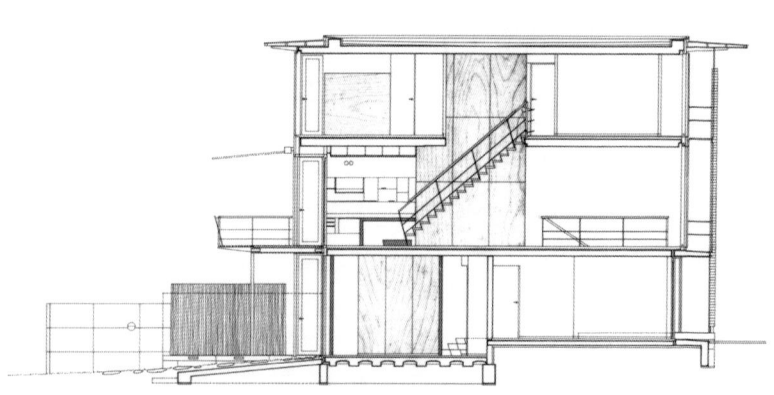

left
House with Studio
Rotterdam, 1989

below
Dedemsvaartweg
The Hague, 1988-1992

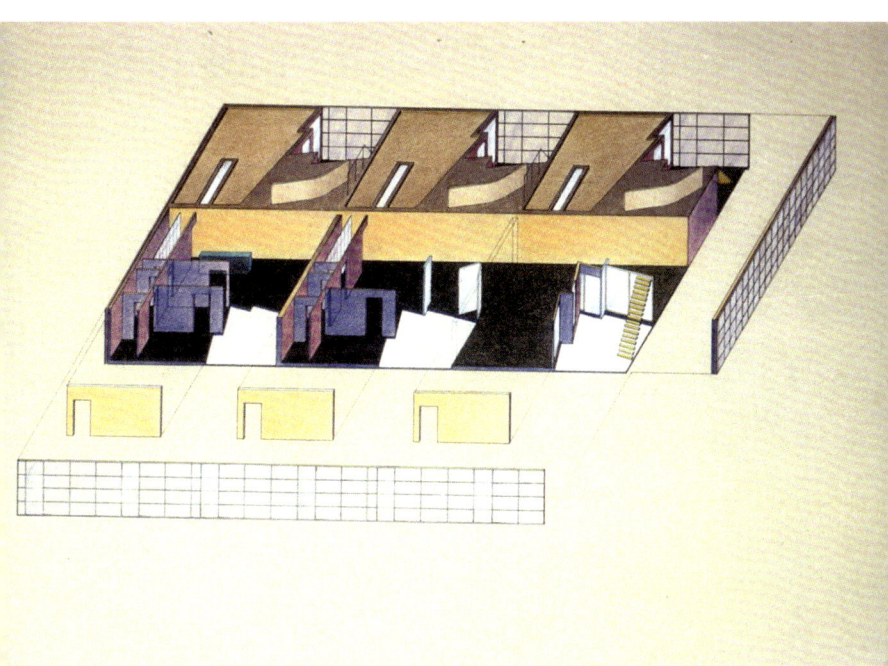

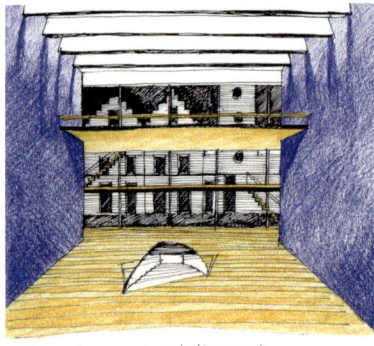

ORIENTATIE OP DE STAD (SLIJKSTRAAT) DE CENTRALE HAL

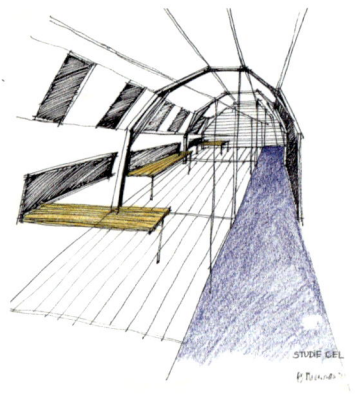

STUDIE CEL

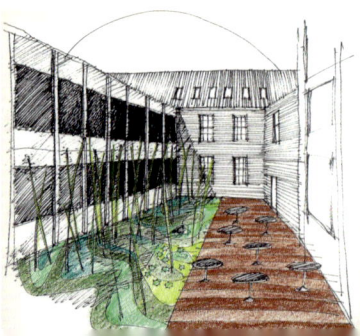

left
Oudemanhuispoort
Amsterdam, 2003

below
Dwelling Nieuw Terbregge area
Rotterdam, 1998

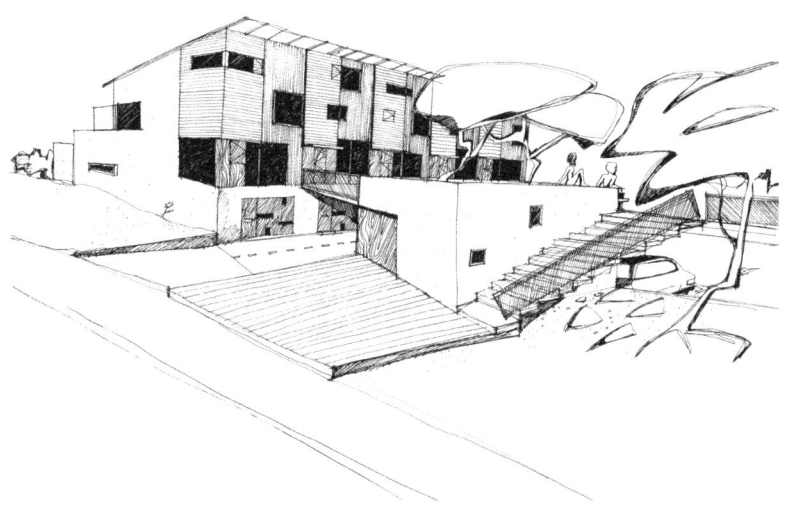

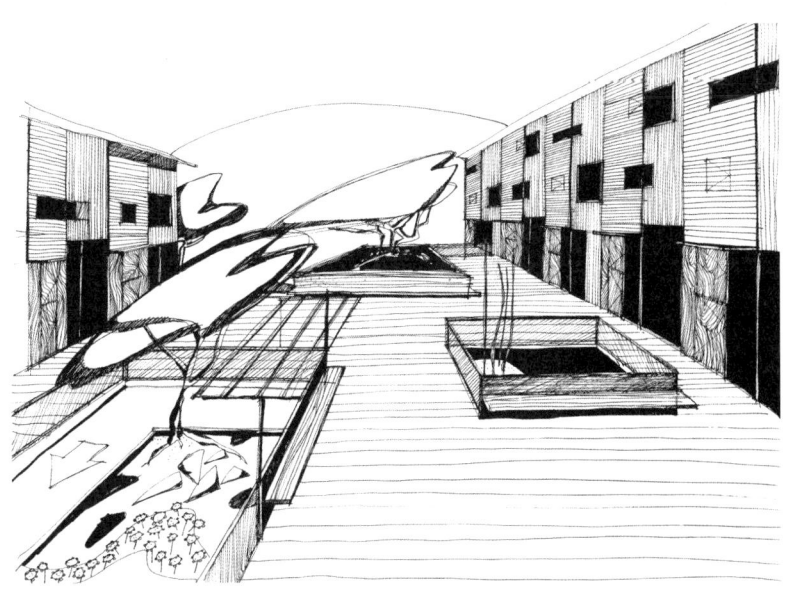

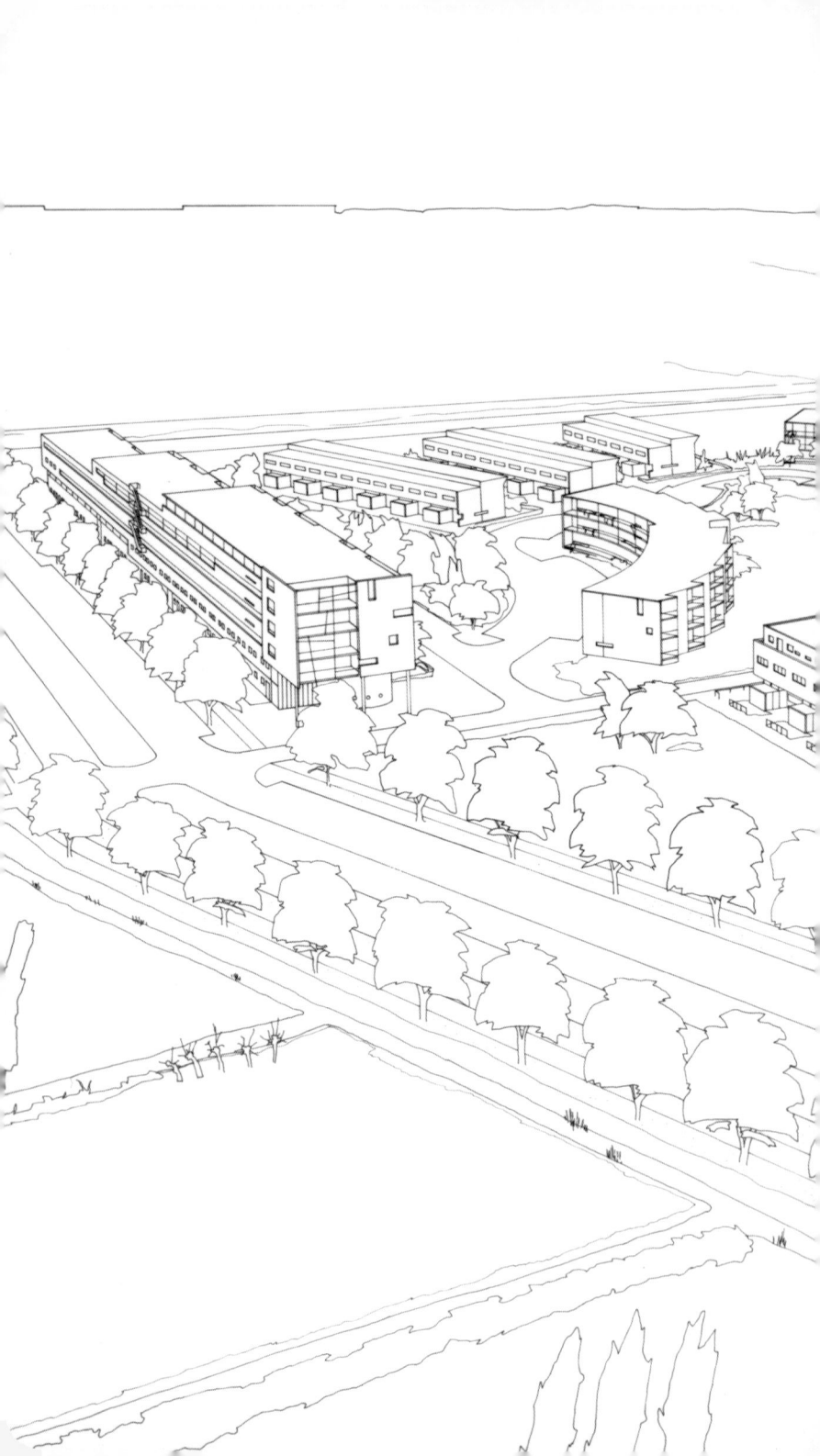

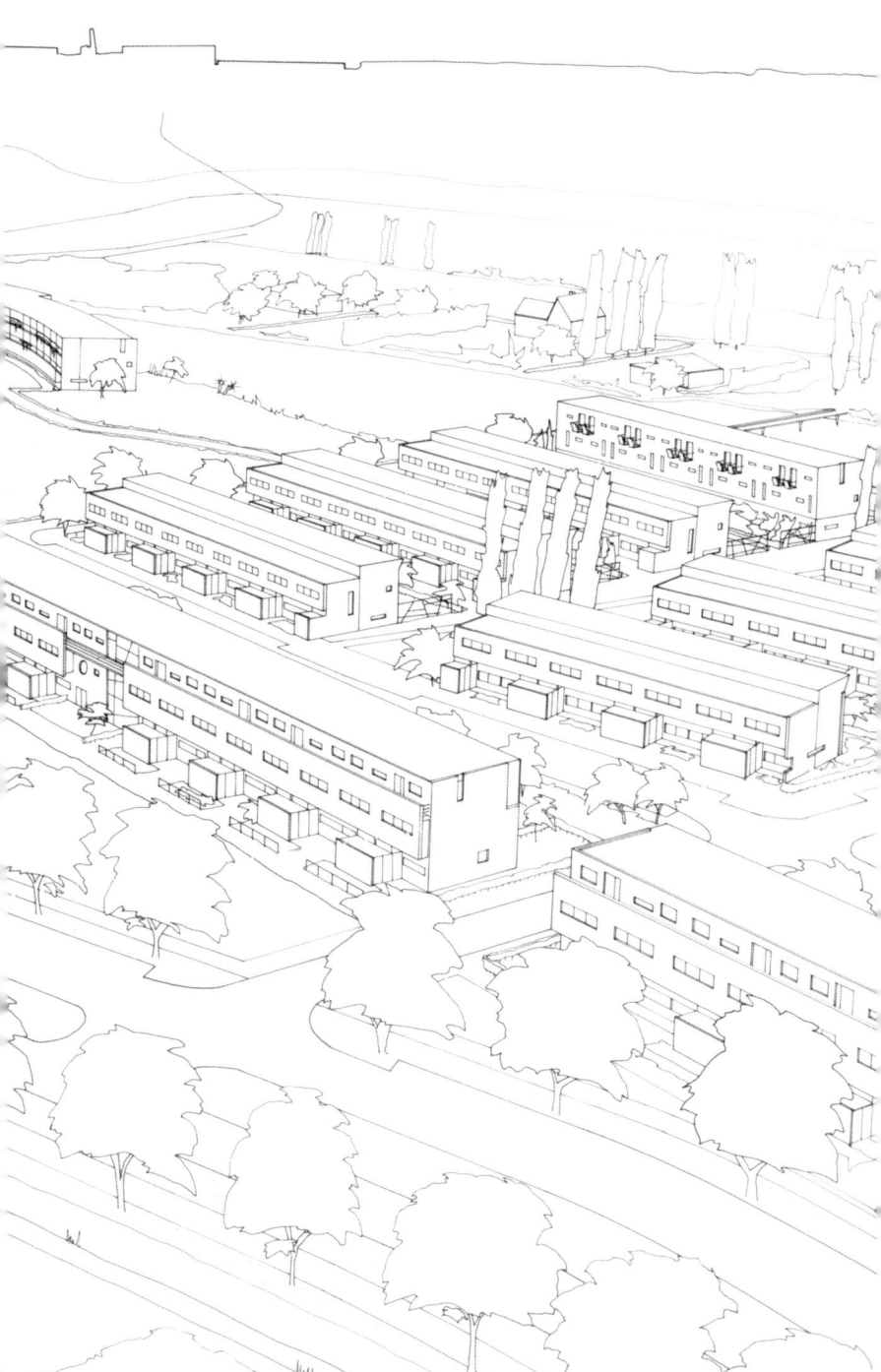

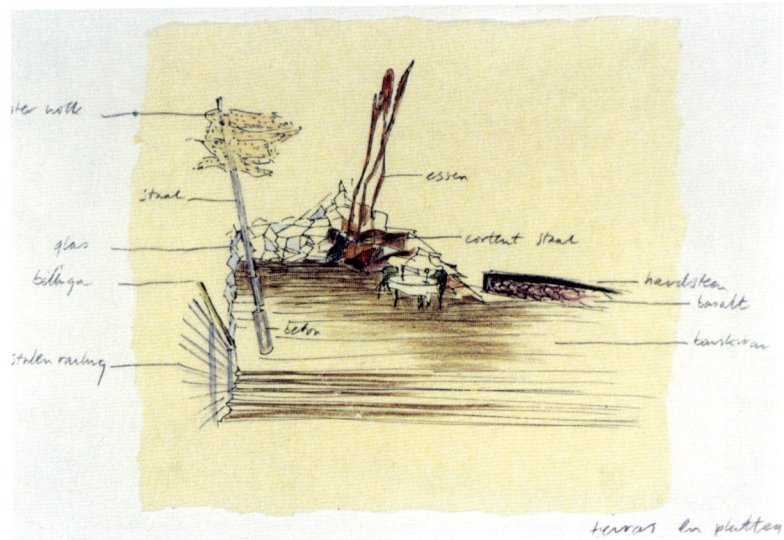

previous pages
Ringvaartplasbuurt Oost Prinsenland
Rotterdam, 1990

above
'Boompjes' Pavilion
Rotterdam, 1989

below, right and following pages
Museum voor Industrie en Samenleving
Kerkrade, 1993

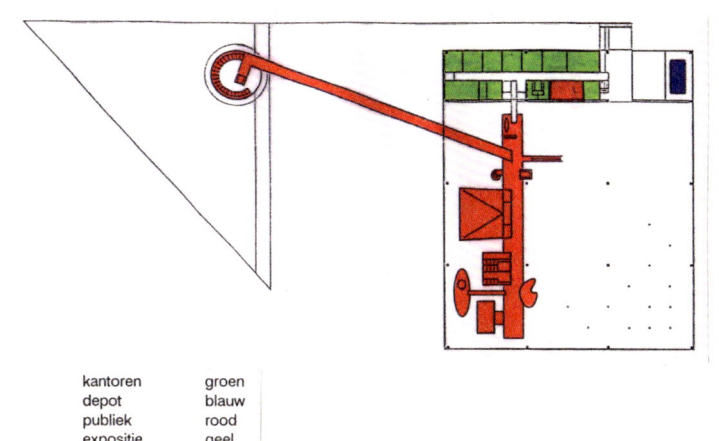

kantoren   groen
depot   blauw
publiek   rood
expositie geel

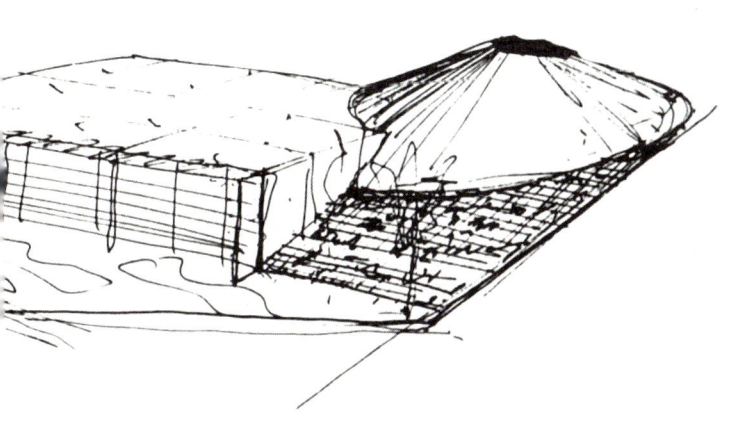

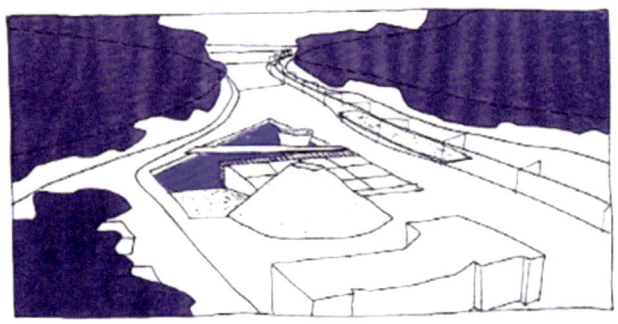
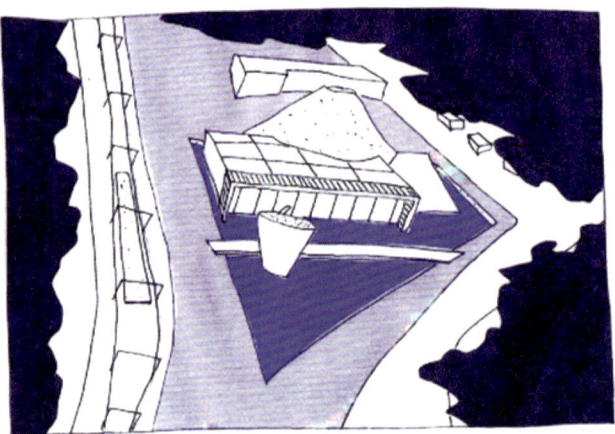

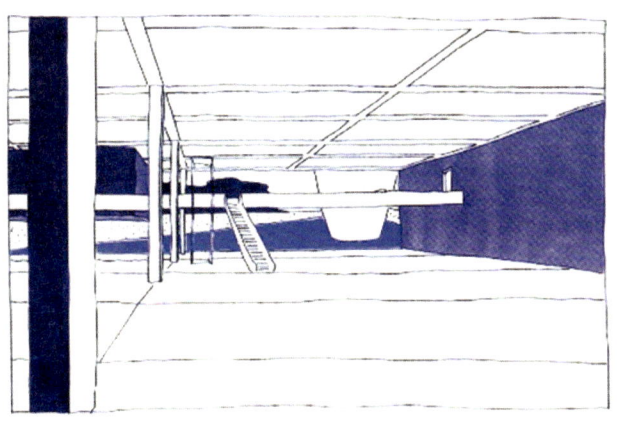

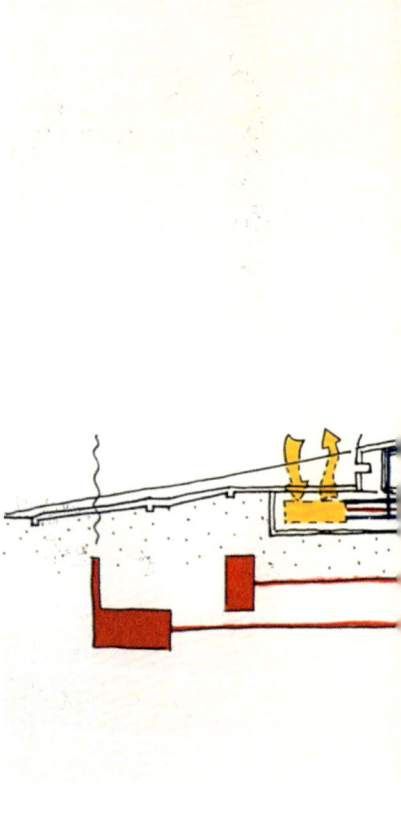

Library Delft University of Technology
Delft, 1993

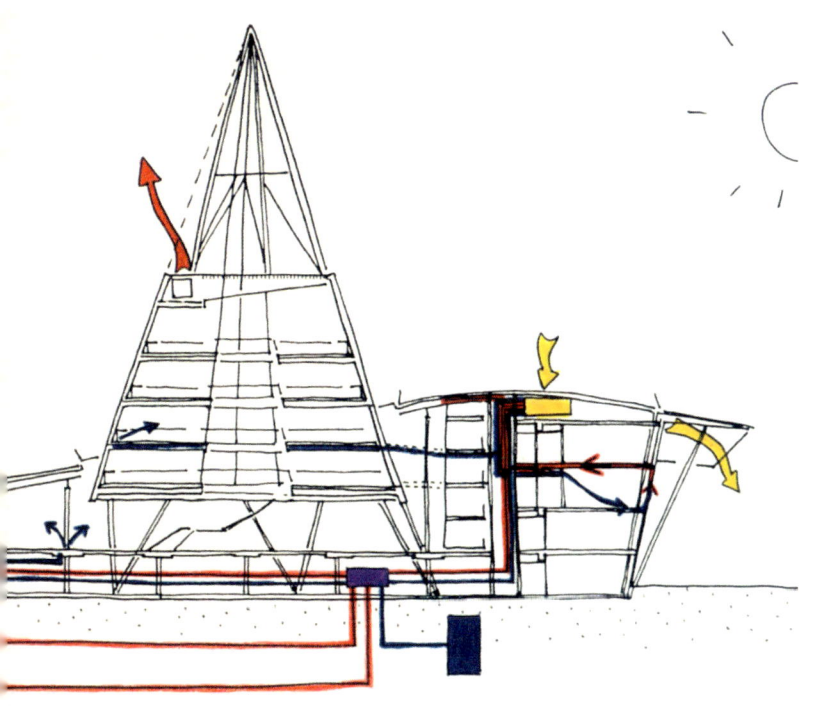

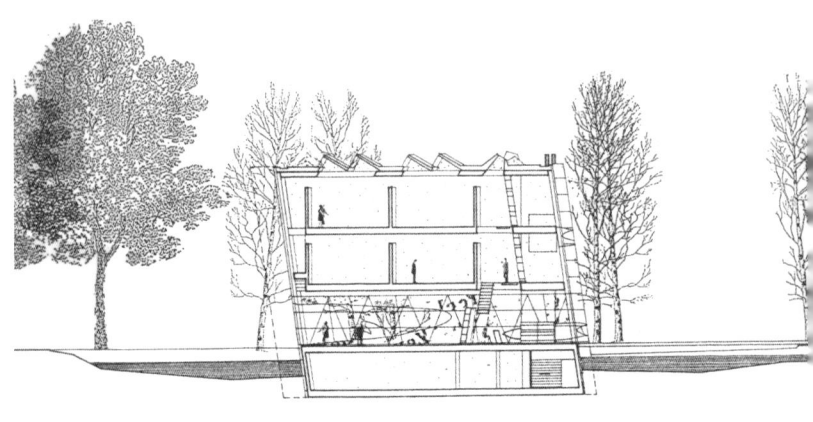

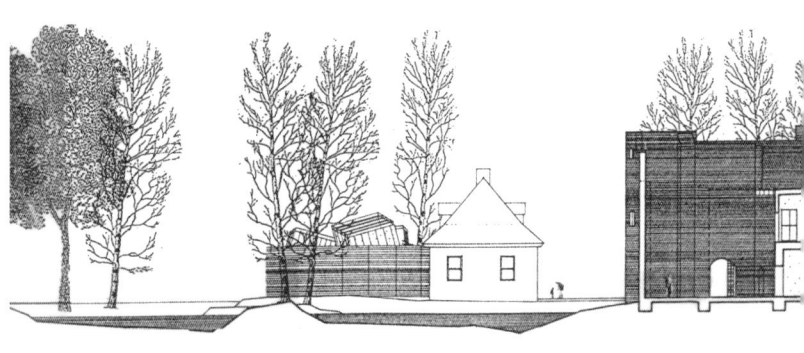

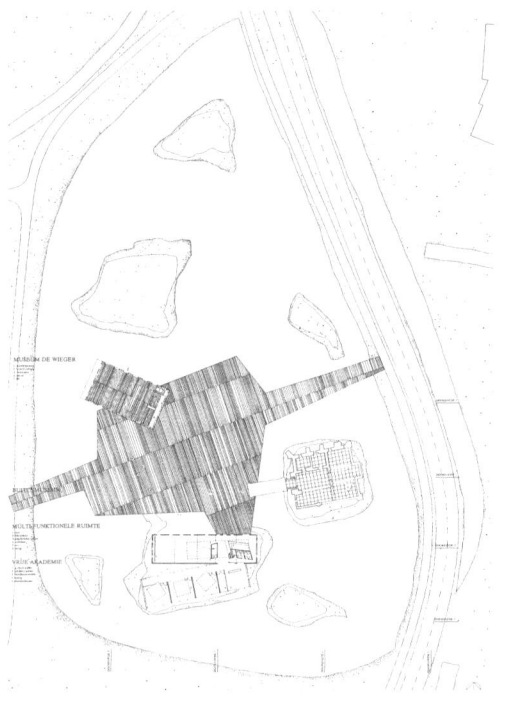

previous and these pages
Castle Ruins Cultural Center
Deurne, 1992

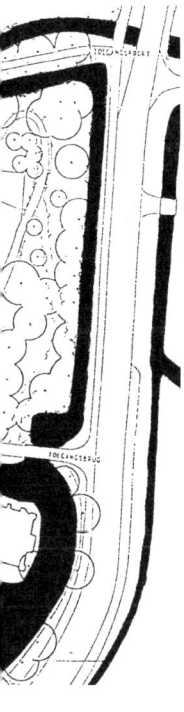
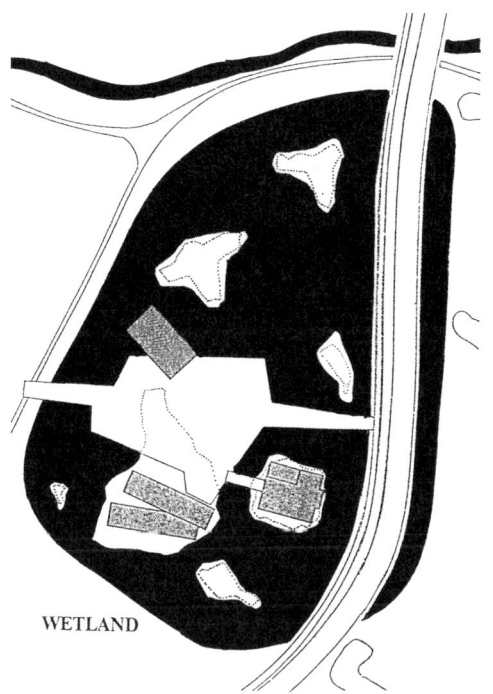

Trust Theater
Amsterdam, 1995-1996

following pages
Parkhotel, extension tower
Rotterdam, 1998-2000

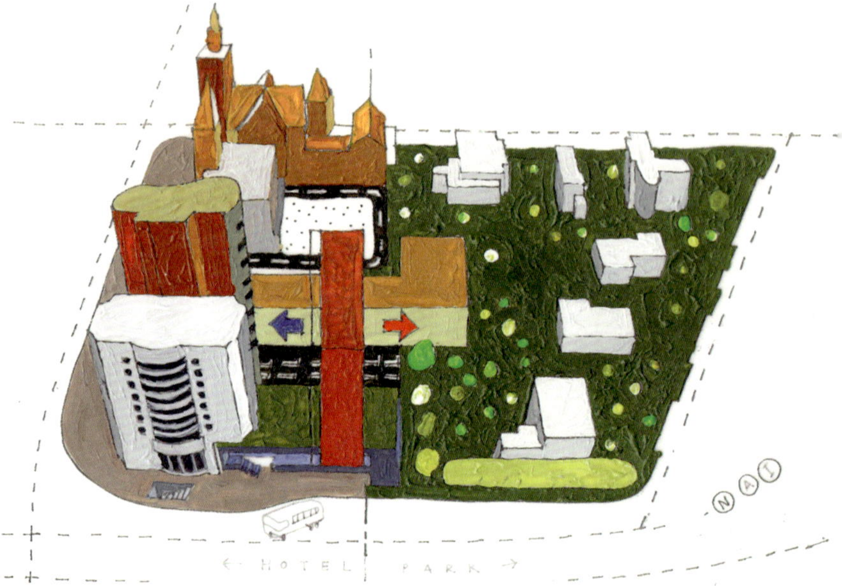

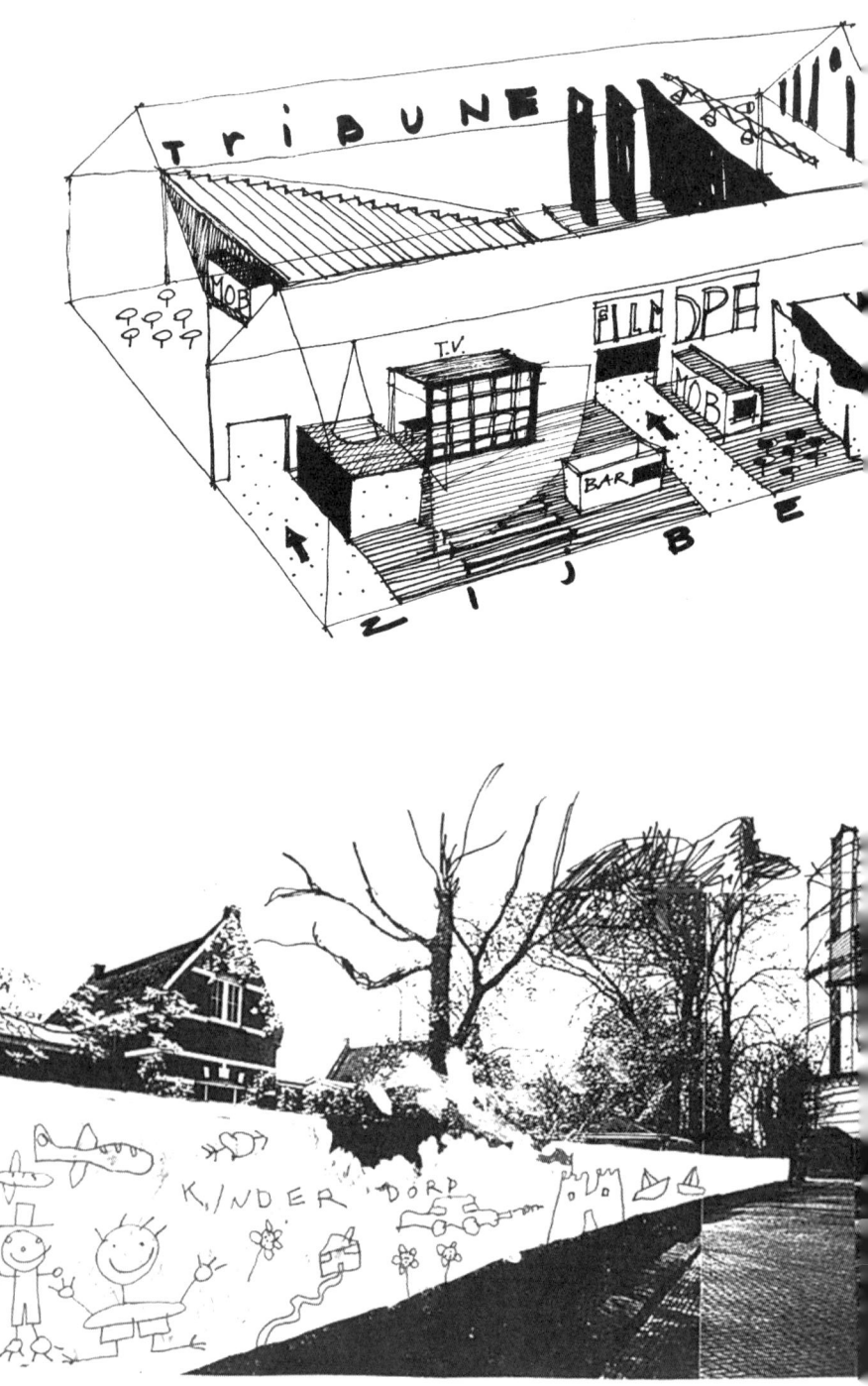

Westergasfabriek site
Amsterdam, 1997

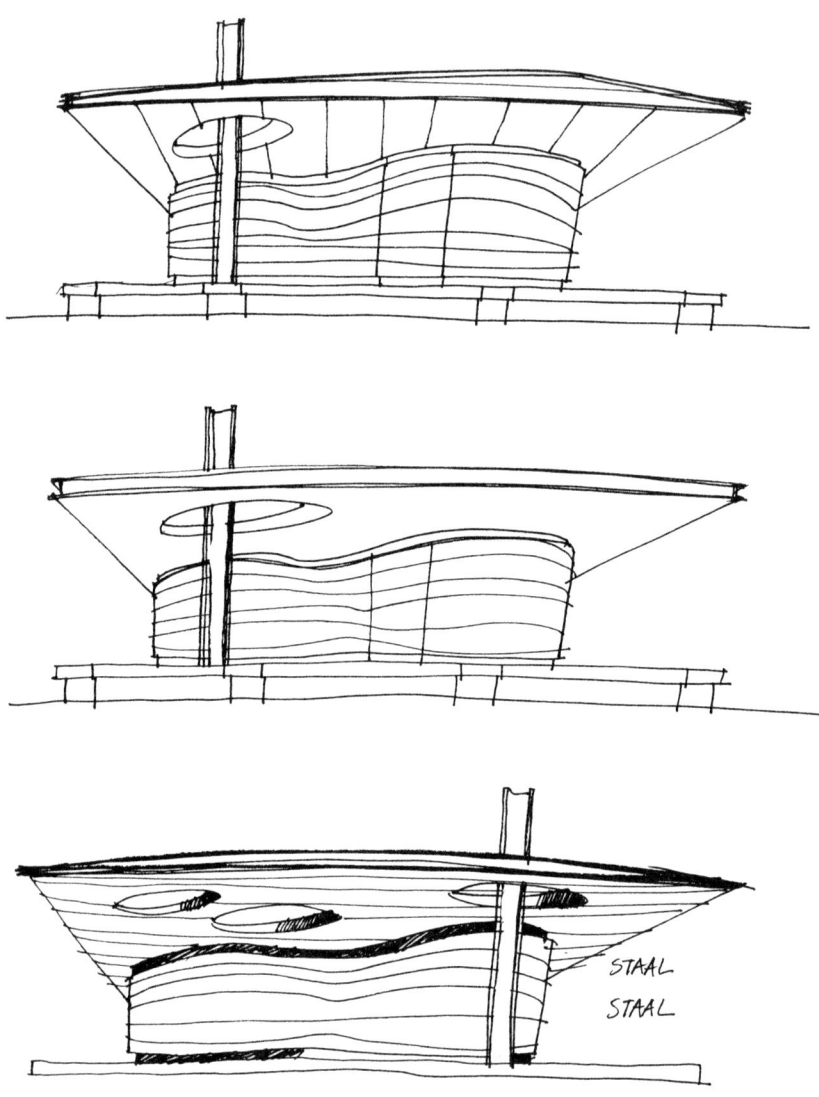

left
St. Mary of the Angels Chapel
Rotterdam, 1998

this page
Montevideo residential tower
Rotterdam, 1999

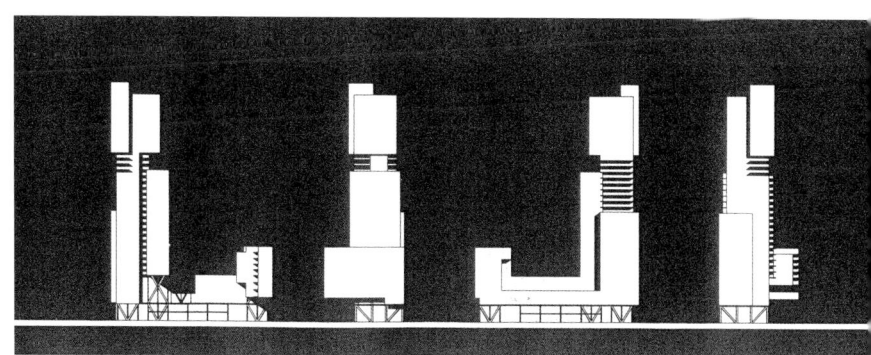

Woonwijk Kanaleneiland
masterplan and design
Utrecht, 2000

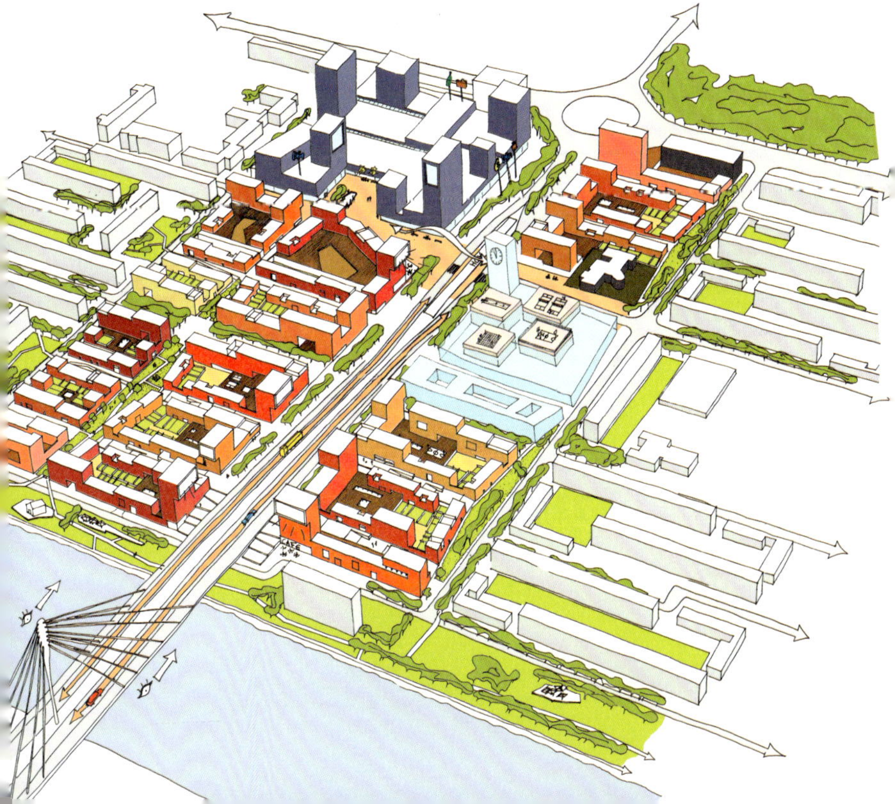

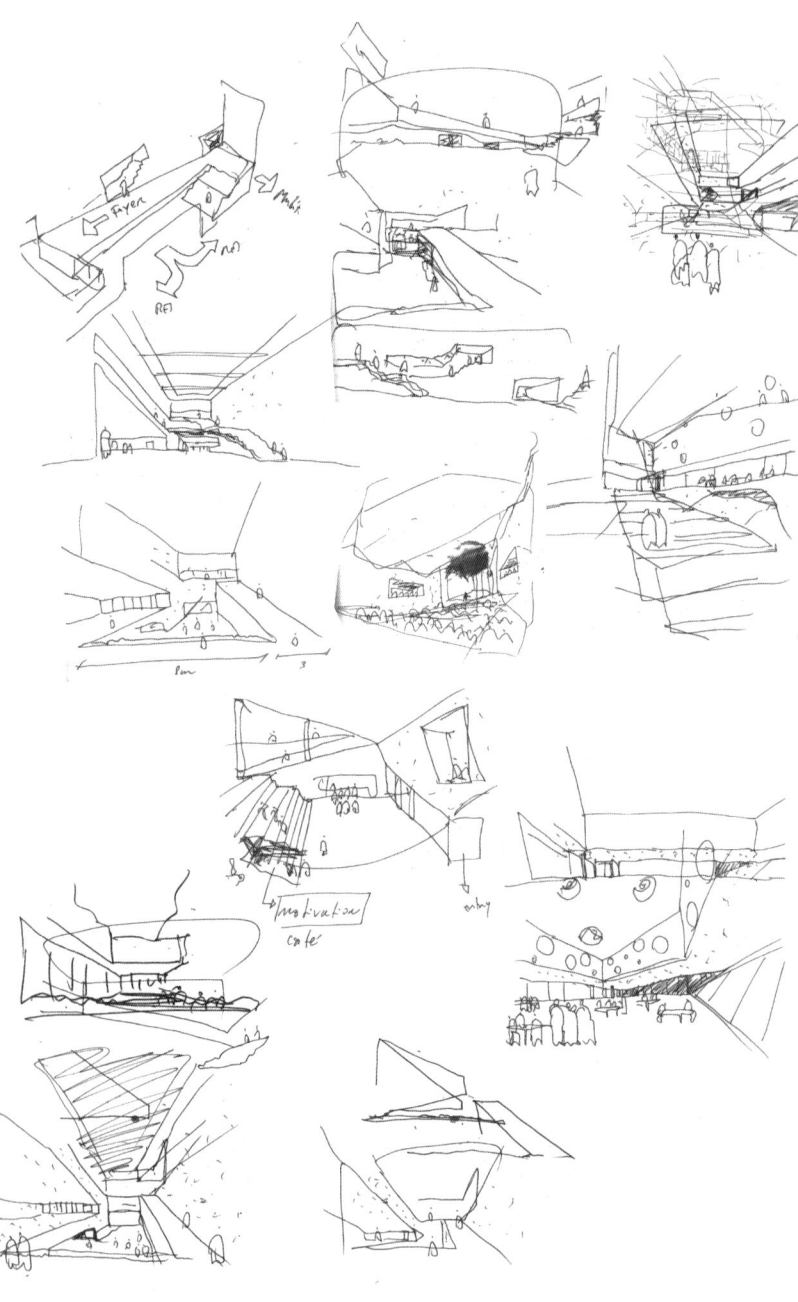

La Llotja Theatre and Conference Centre
Lleida, 2004

BBC Headquarters
Glasgow, 2001

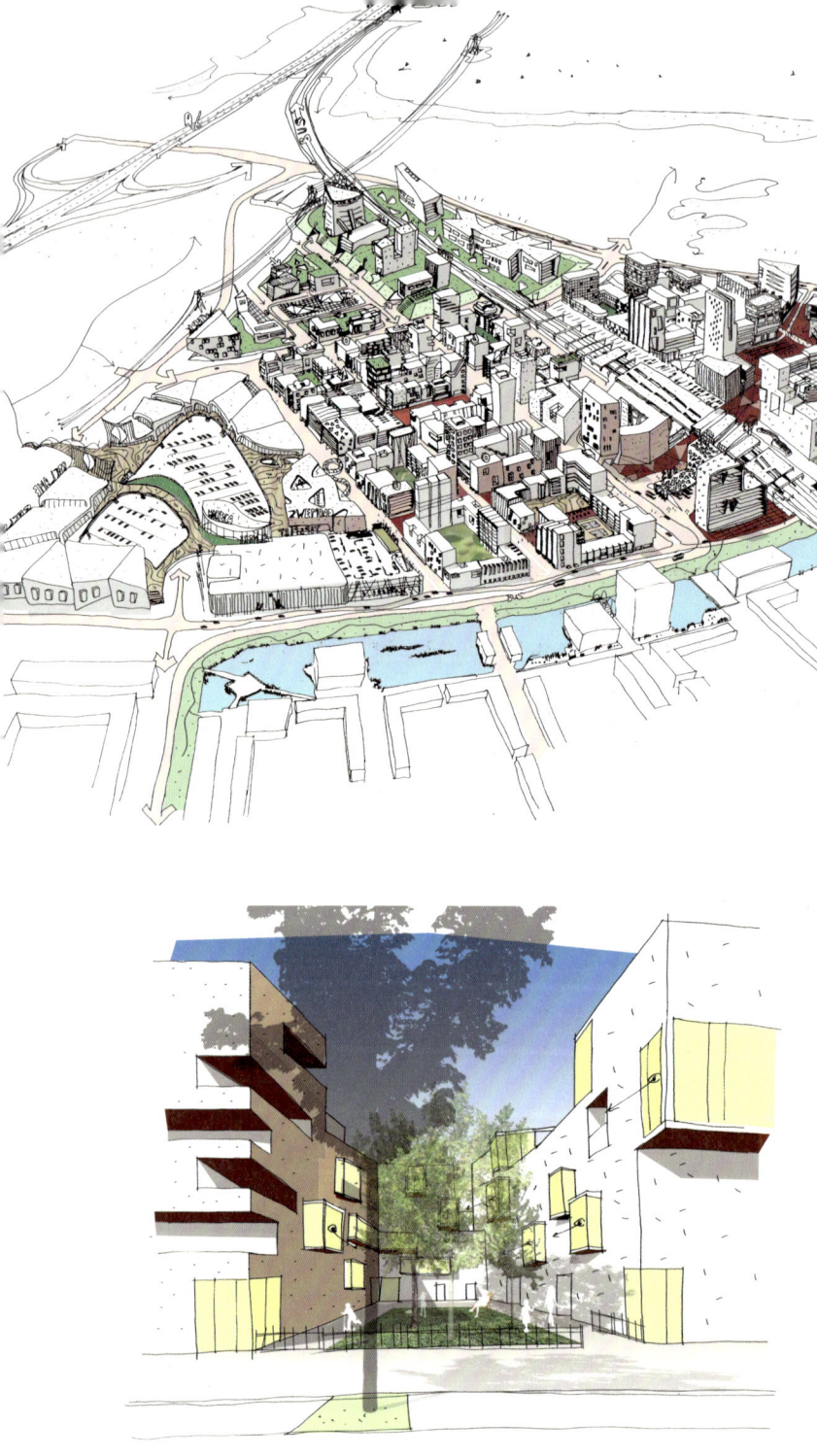

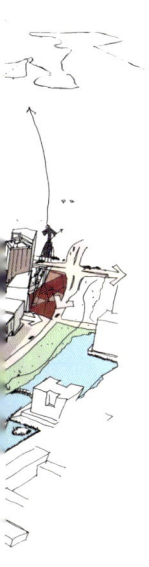

Olympiakwartier urban planning
Almere, 2002

these pages
Amphion Theater
Doetinchem, 2006

following pages
Palace of Justice
Cordoba, 2006

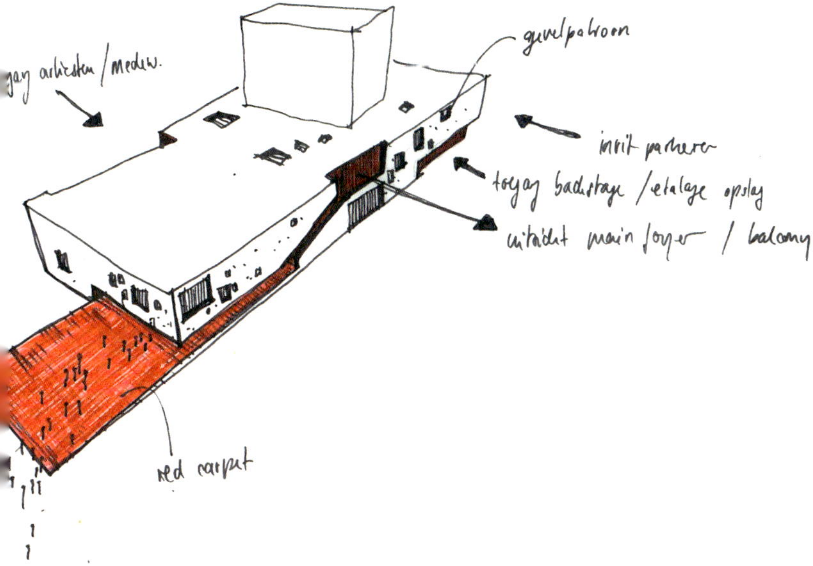

gay artiesten/medew.

gevelpatroon

inrit parkeren

toyay backstage / etalage opslag

uitrit main foyer / balcony

red carpet

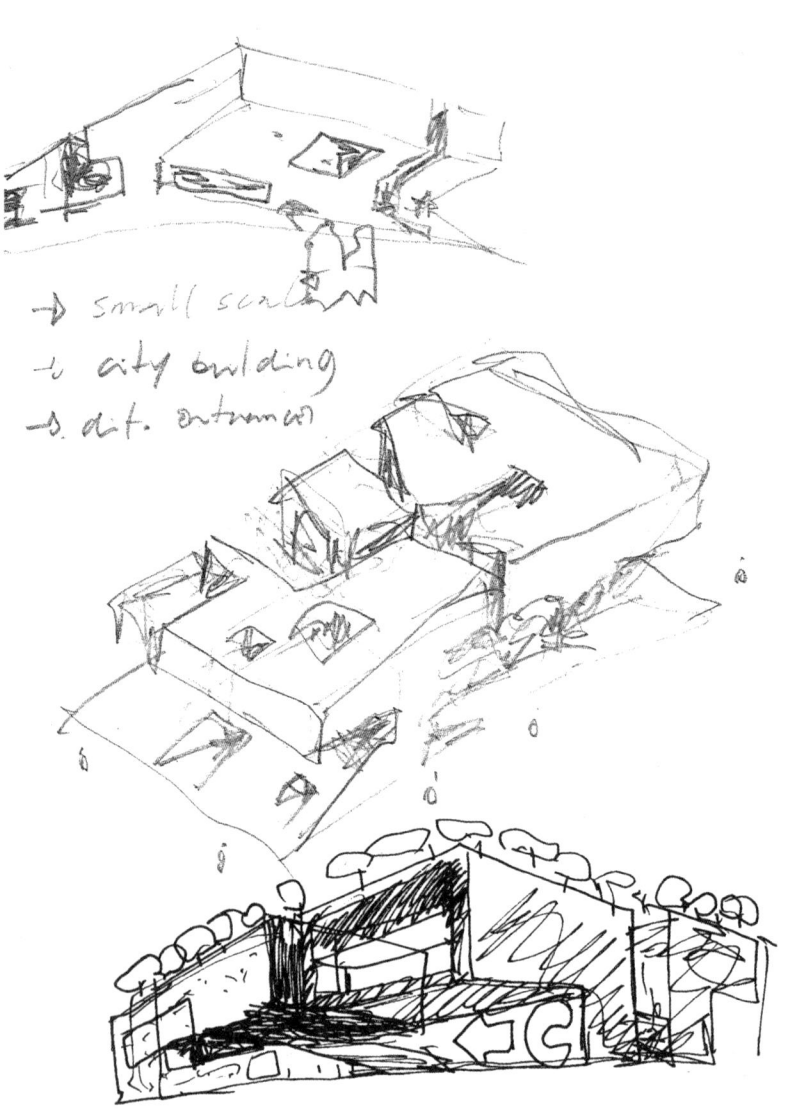

→ small scale
→ city building
→ dif. entrances

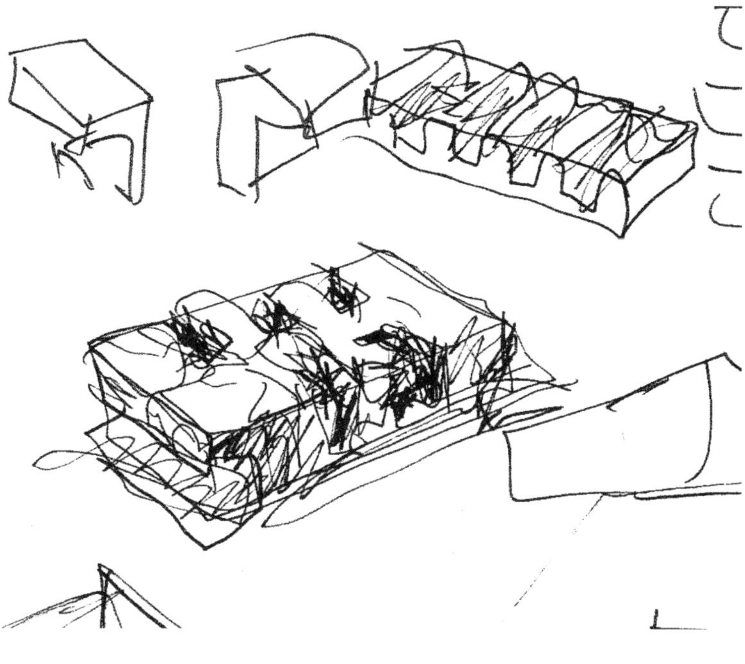

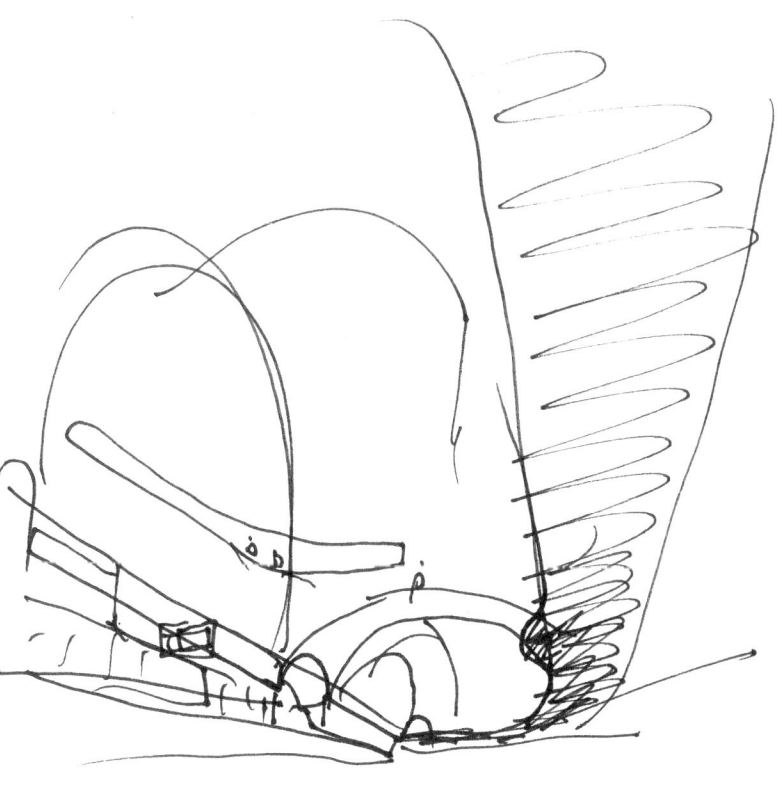

Municipal Offices and Train Station
Delft, 2006

Mid Manhattan library · Fifth Avenue · St

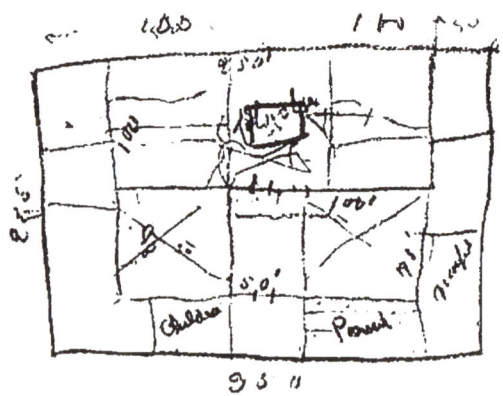

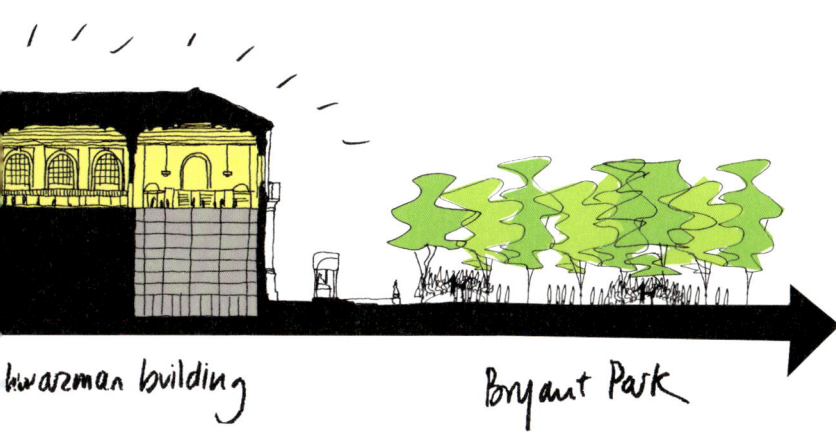

New York Public Library Midtown Campus
New York, 2015

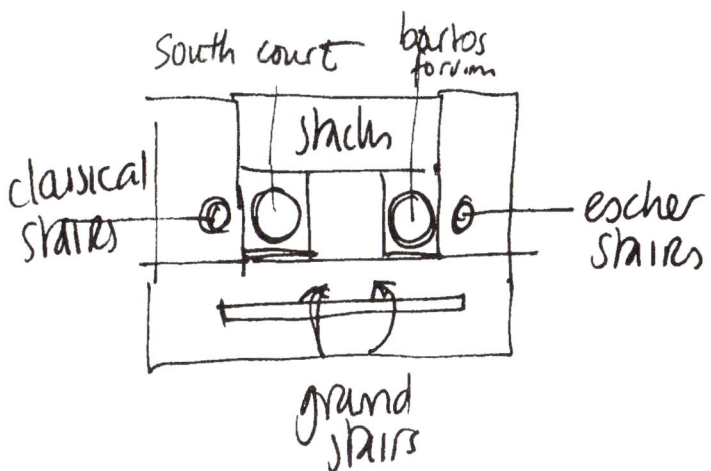

Nationaal Landbouw Museum
Beesd, 2007

Tainan Public Library
Tainan, 2017

Recording

The power of memory and the material culture of the places where the project develops and is given a shape clearly emerge in the office's working methods. Its solutions often retain more or less complete traces of certain external stimuli. The underlying criteria bound up with images, sensations, existing structures and artifacts are evoked in contemporary and completely original terms. Mecanoo's architecture, with its timely vocabulary, frequently enables communities to preserve and evoke memories without nostalgia, arousing and reinforcing a strong, sensitive, iconic, emotional and intellectual identity. This reinterpretation of signs is evident when the practice works on a built-up site. The traces of the past are recorded, reinterpreted sensitively, and restored to life in the project.

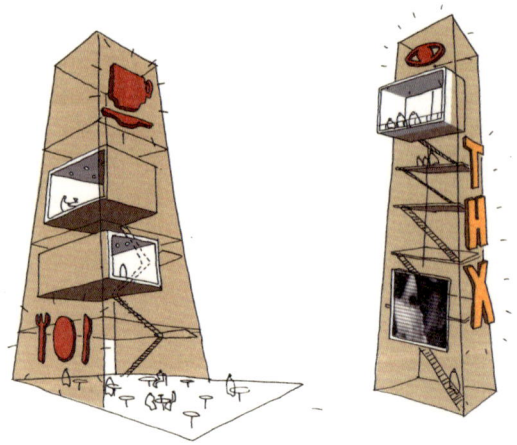

Retail Park Square
Westermaat
Hengelo, 1999

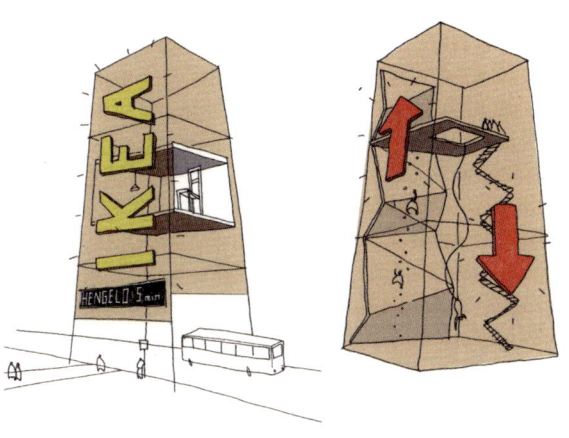

Westergasfabriek site
Amsterdam, 1997

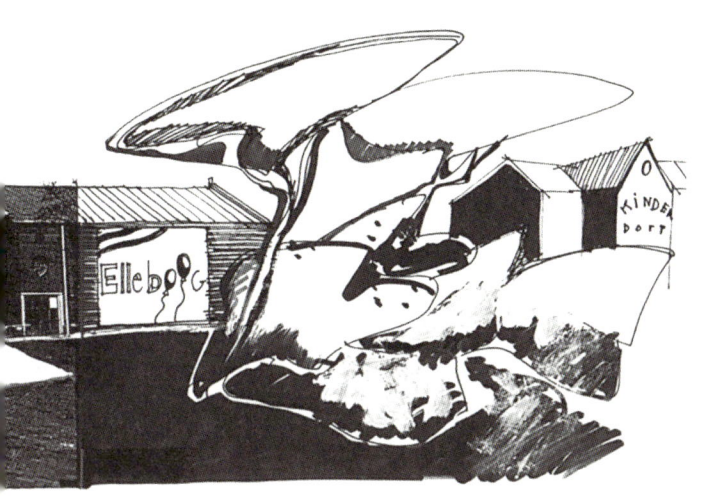

Trust Theater
Amsterdam,
1995-1996

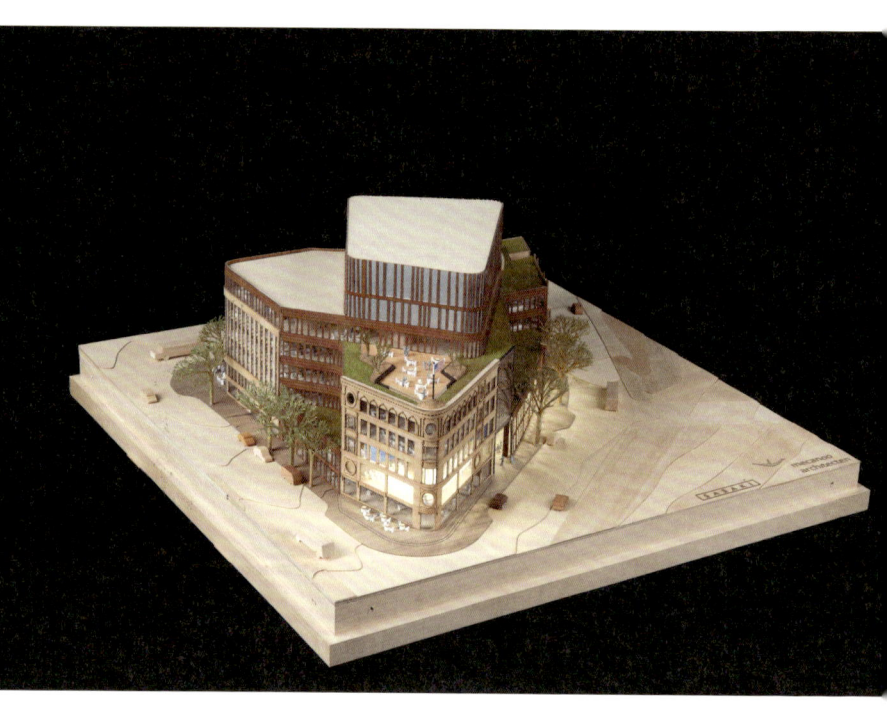

Bruce C. Bolling
Municipal Building
Boston, 2011

BLUE STORE
RUGS
OIL

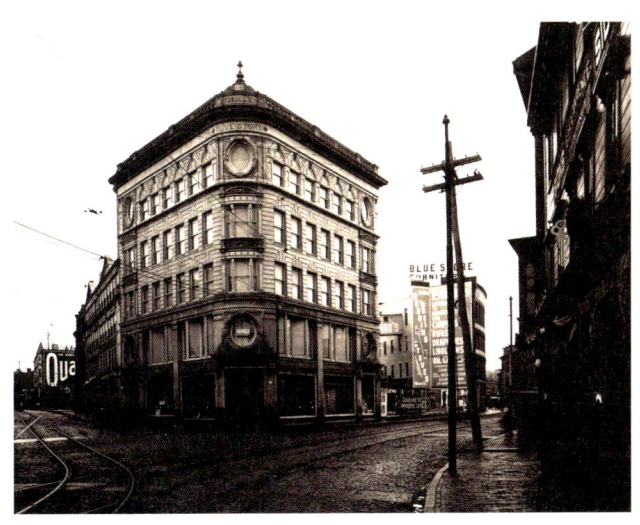

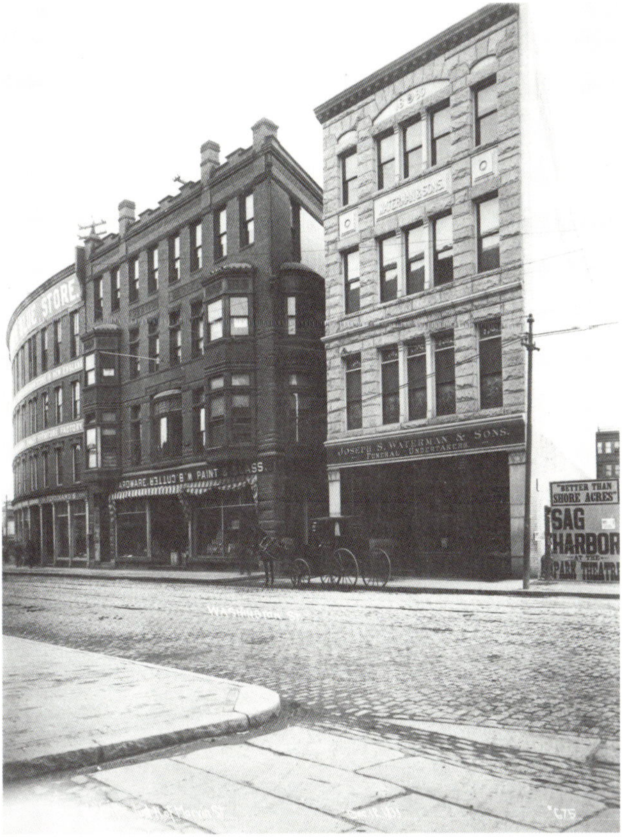
STORE.
WATERMAN & SONS
W B CUTLER
PAINT
JOSEPH S. WATERMAN & SONS.
FUNERAL UNDERTAKERS
"BETTER THAN SHORE ACRES"
SAG
HARBOR
AT THE
PARK
WASHINGTON ST.

National Kaohsiung
Center for the Arts
Kaohsiung, 2007

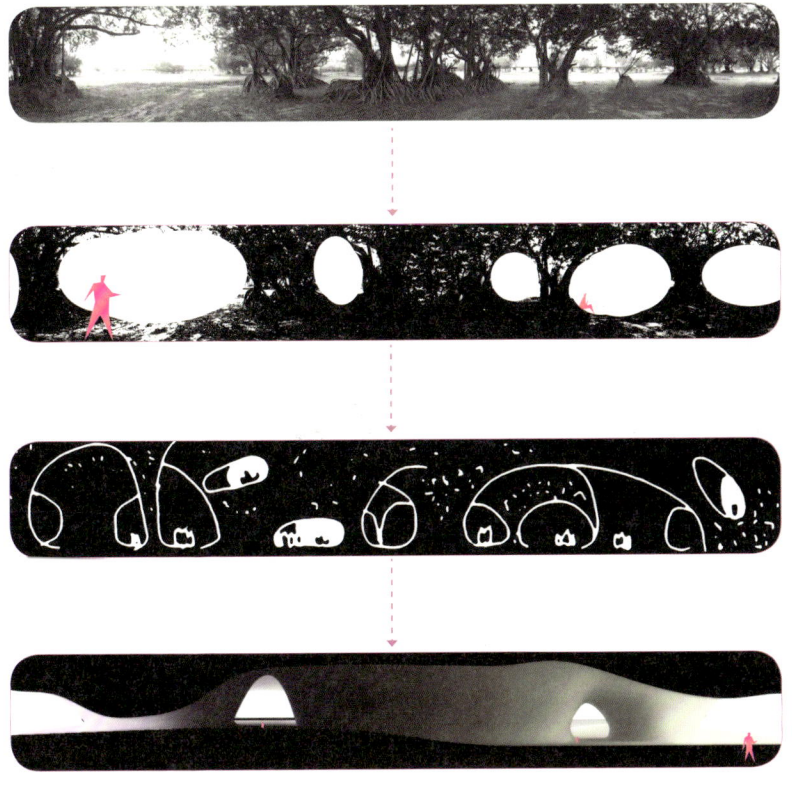

these and following pages
House with studio
Rotterdam, 1991-2006
Photographs
by Francine Houben

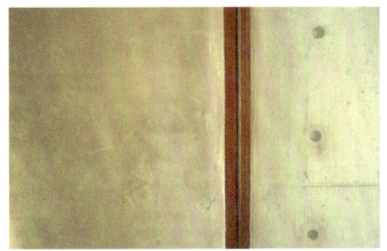

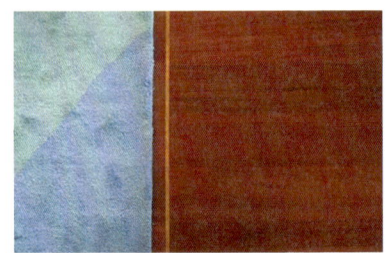

Diagramming

Mecanoo principally designs public architecture, spaces and buildings for people. To do this, the process has to analyze and stress its functions, the relations between them and all the different kinds of flows that take place inside and outside the architectural complex. These observations give rise to a series of singular drawings: diagrams, schemes, signs, lettering, representations with a purely graphic character. The elaboration of this stage of the process is epitomized in a set of lines and notes that, connected and/or sequentially related, describe the operations that can be performed around the architectural machine or master plan. In each case they foster the potential for interpreting and exploring the project through research that is never static.

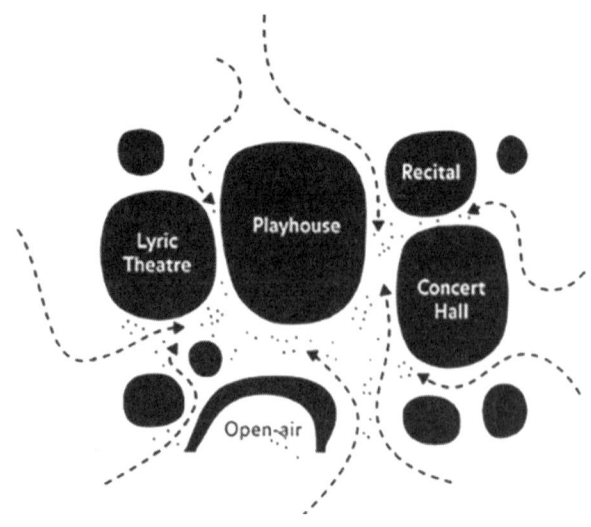

left
**National Kaohsiung
Center for the Arts**
Kaohsiung, 2007

below
**Retail Park Square
Westermaat**
Hengelo, 1999

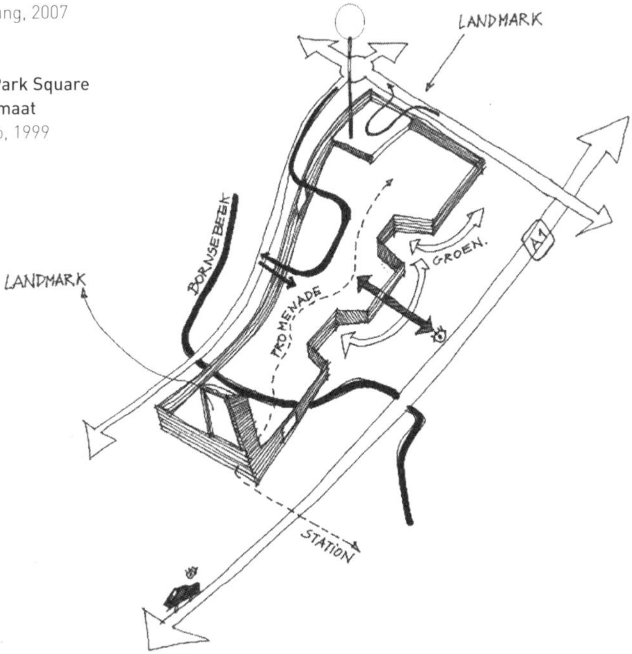

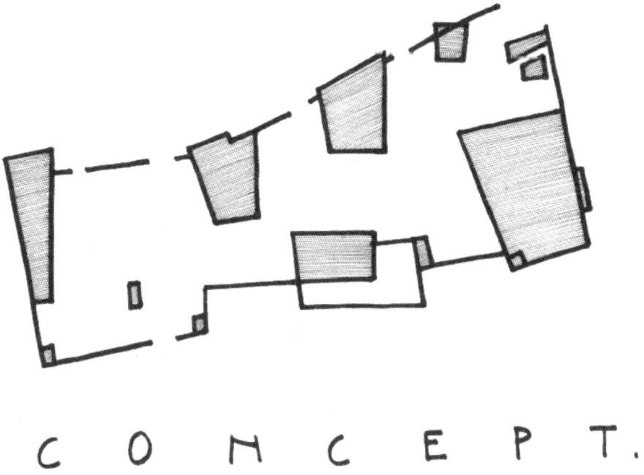

CONCEPT.

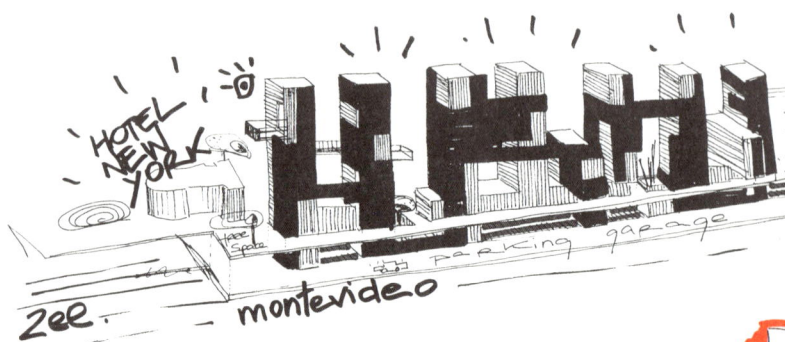

these and following pages
Montevideo residential tower
Rotterdam, 1999

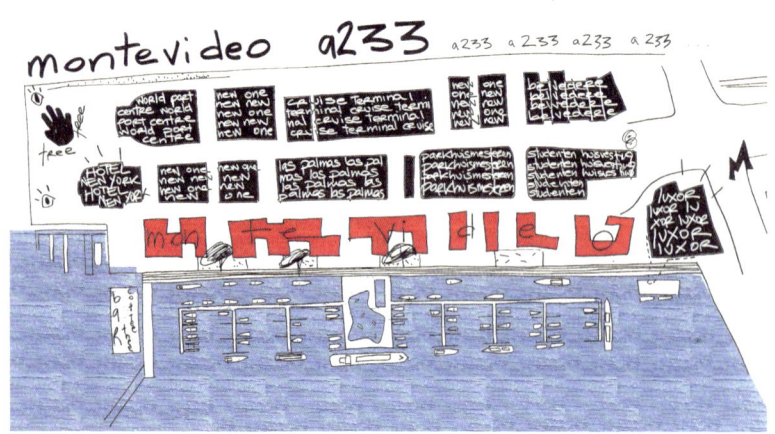

233.

a233

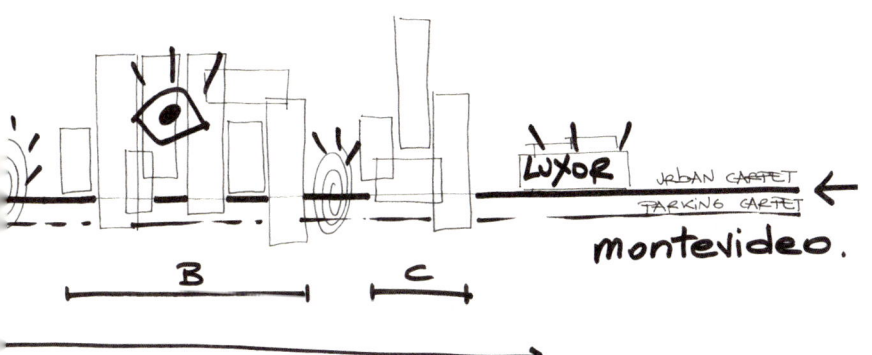
montevideo.

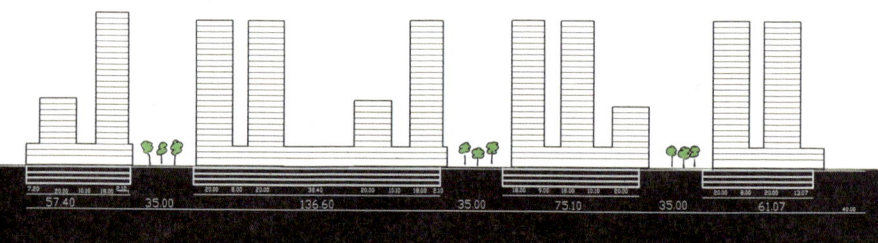

WISSEL
BOVENWERELD

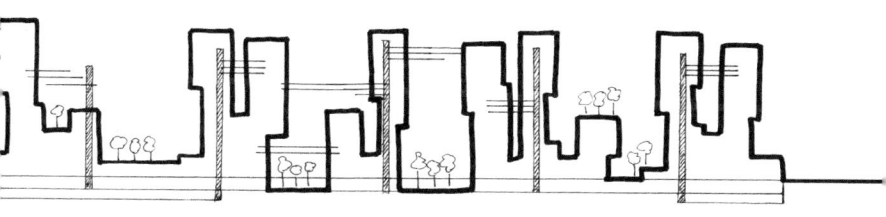

ONDERWERELD
WERKING

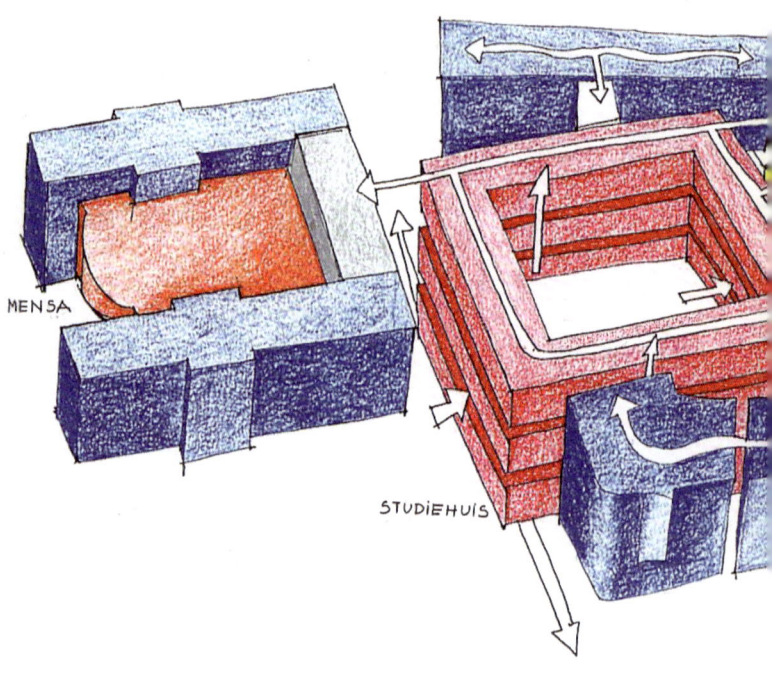

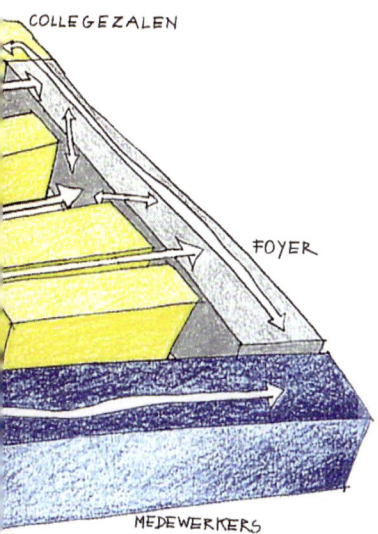

Oudemanhuispoort
Amsterdam, 2003

below
**Kaap Skil, Maritime
and Beachcombers Museum**
Oudeschild, 2007

above and right
National Historic Museum
Arnhem, 2007

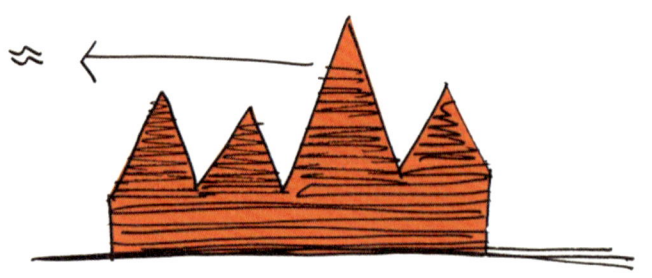

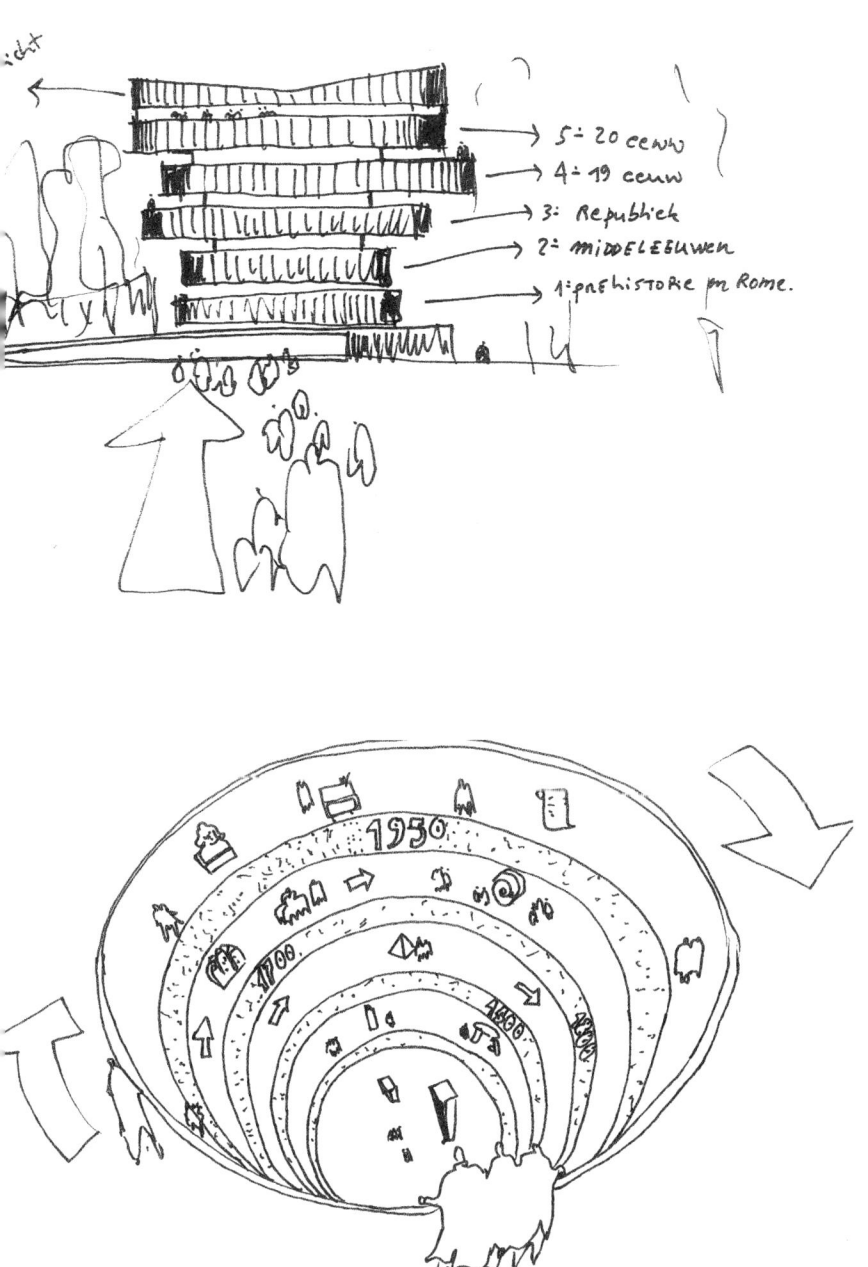

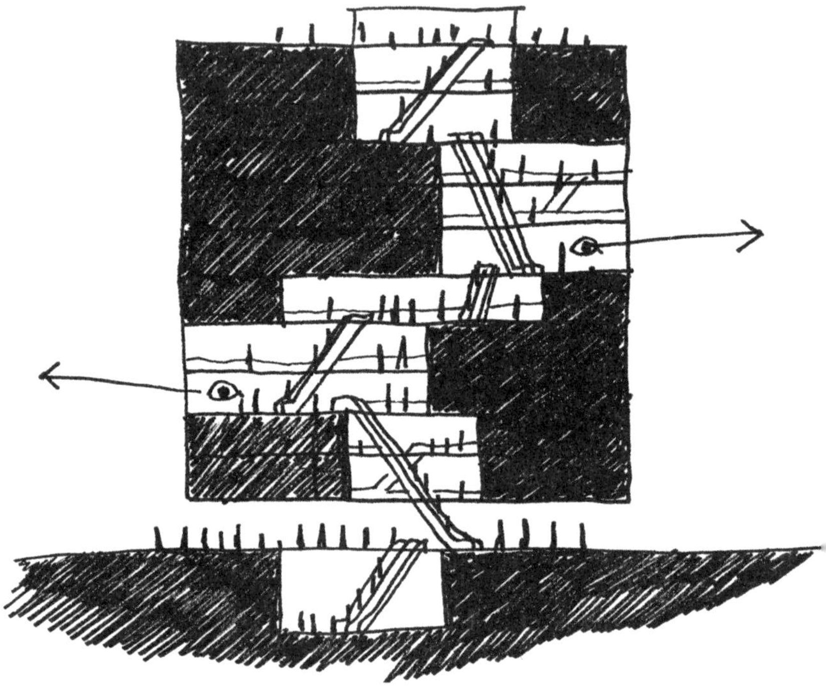

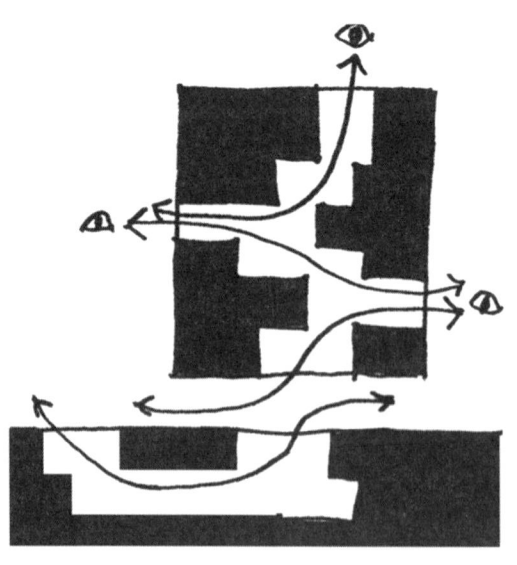

left
Library of Birmingham
Birmingham, 2008

below
City Hall Redevelopment
Rotterdam, 2009

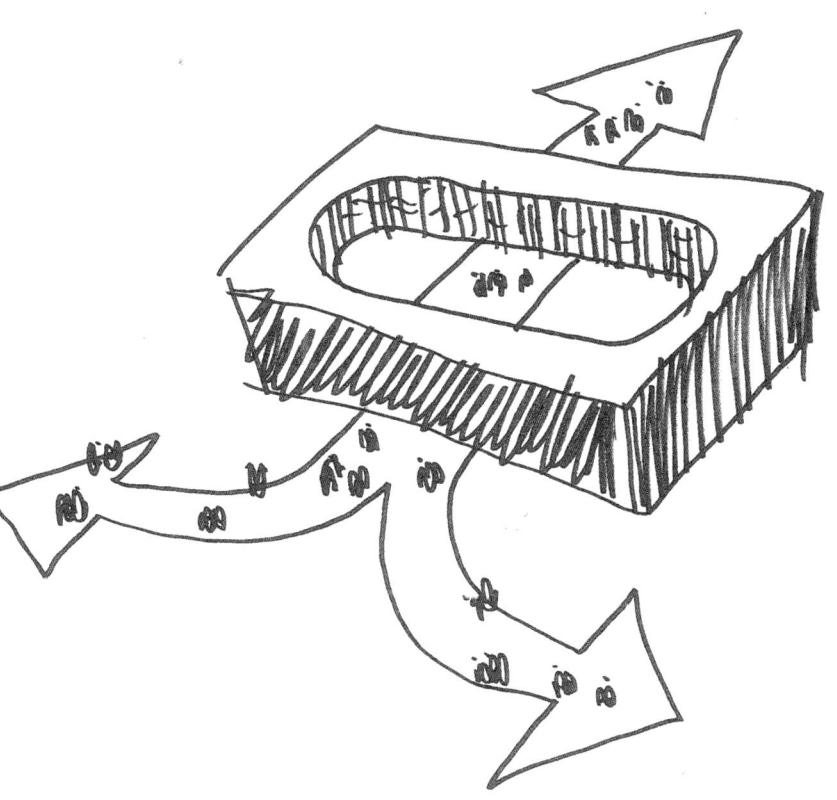

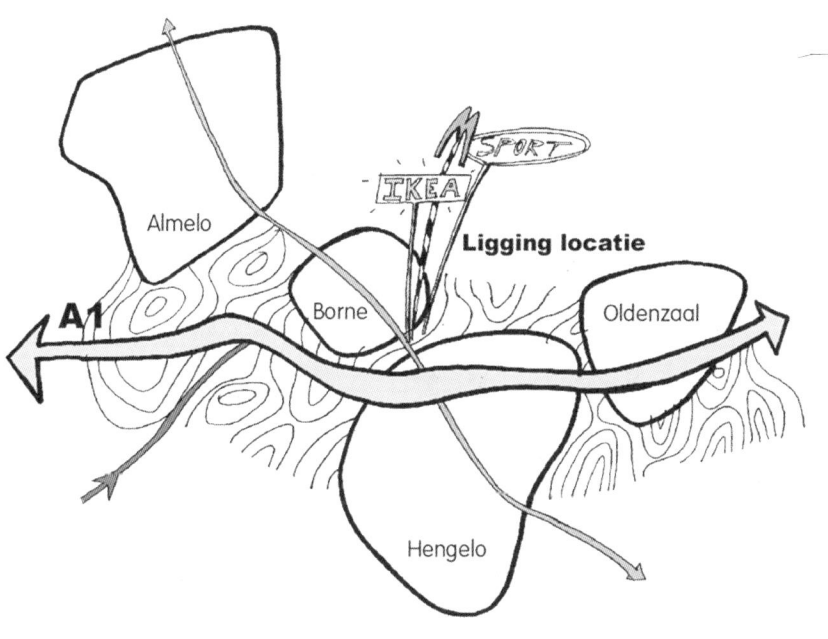

left
Ringvaartplasbuurt Oost
Rotterdam, 1990

above
Retail Park Square Westermaat
Hengelo, 1999

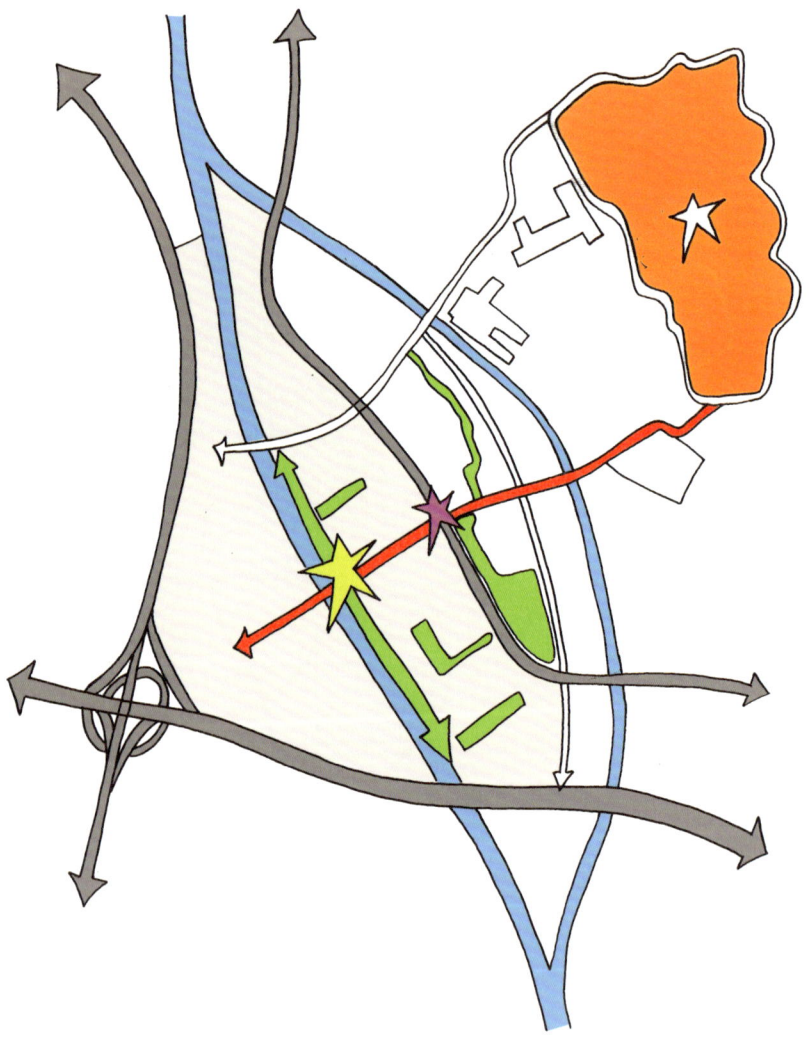

these pages
Woonwijk Kanaleneiland masterplan and design
Utrecht, 2000

following pages
Thamesmead Regeneration
London, 2015

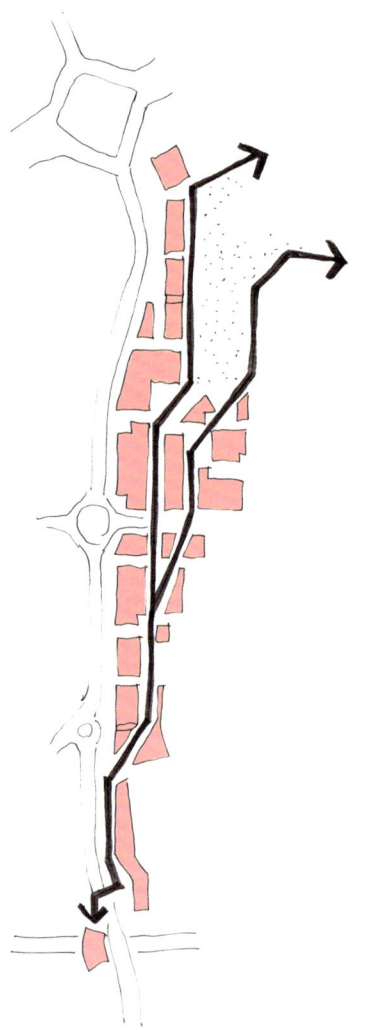
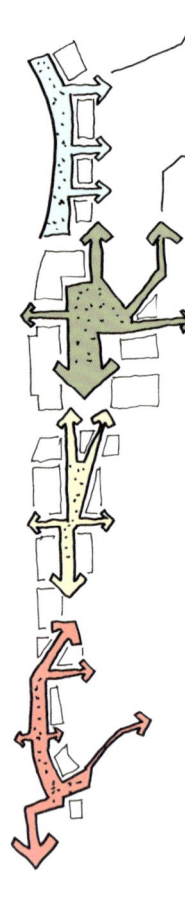

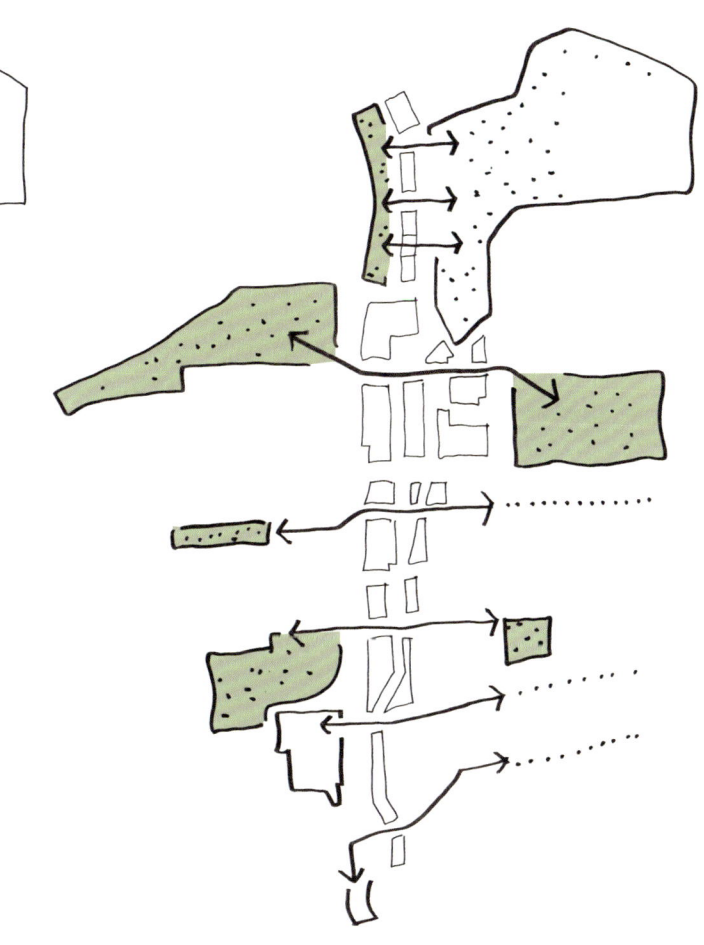

Assembling

In observing the office's work, a feature emerges that may not be central to the process of conception but is of interest as expressing the idea embodied in the design. It is found in some compositions created using techniques of collage, or more properly assembly, images printed, cut out, juxtaposed and supplemented with drawings done by hand or computer. What might seem like an anachronistic approach conceals an extraordinary ability to bring together and harmoniously compose different phases of the conceptual process, seeking to verify their potential and balance, variations and stimuli, proportions and relations.

These representations become instruments of the research that brings the architecture to life: in it people, natural elements, traces and memories are superimposed and stratified. Mecanoo's design approach is open and ready to absorb the signs recorded in a process of listening. Here this stratification begins to shape up and is expressed on paper.

below
Netherlands Open Air Museum
Arnhem, 1995

right
Westergasfabriek site
Amsterdam, 1997

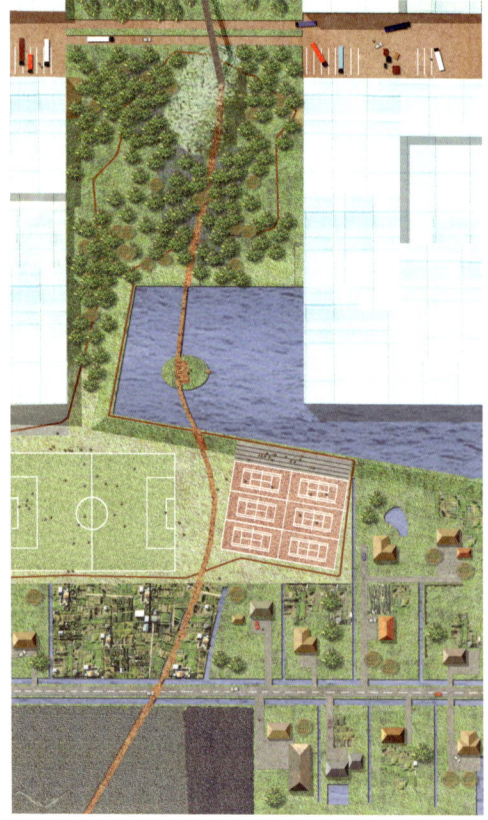

previous pages
'Boompjes' Pavilion
Rotterdam, 1989

these pages
Glass Village
Rotterdam, Gouda and The Hague
(Zuidplaspolder), 2001

these pages
Castle Ruins Cultural Center
Deurne, 1992

following pages
Museum voor Industrie en Samenleving
Kerkrade, 1993

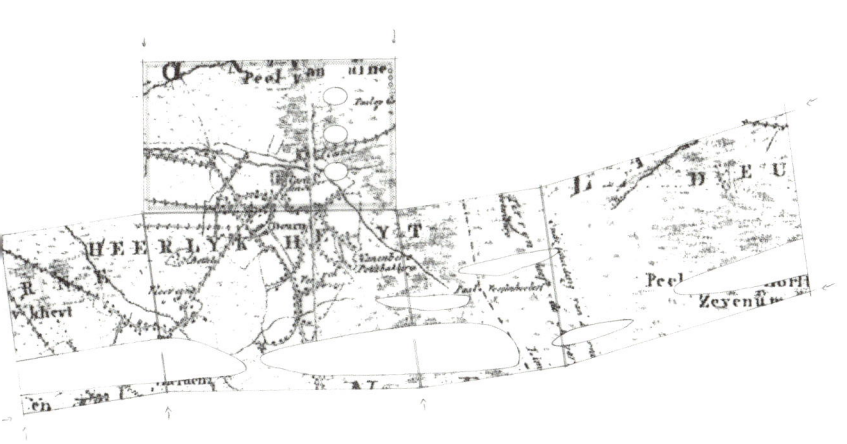

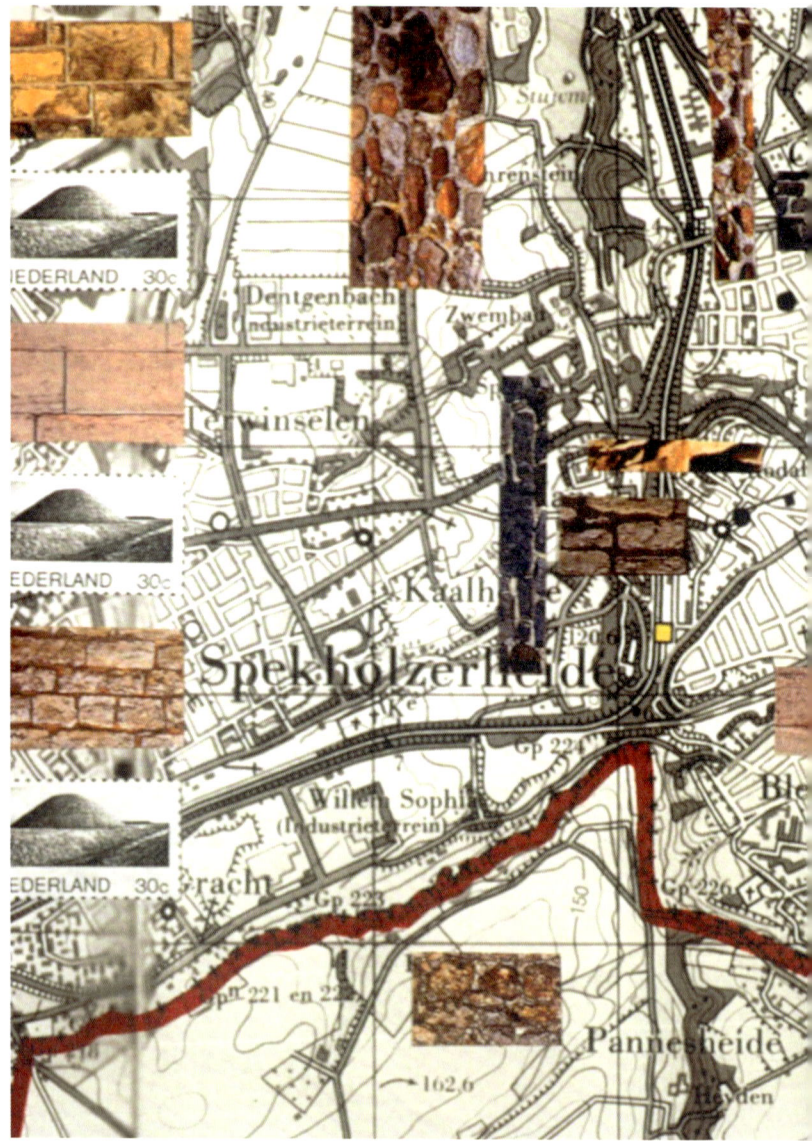

these pages
Almere Hout Masterplan
Almere, 2002-2004

following pages
Ringvaartplasbuurt Oost
Rotterdam, 1990

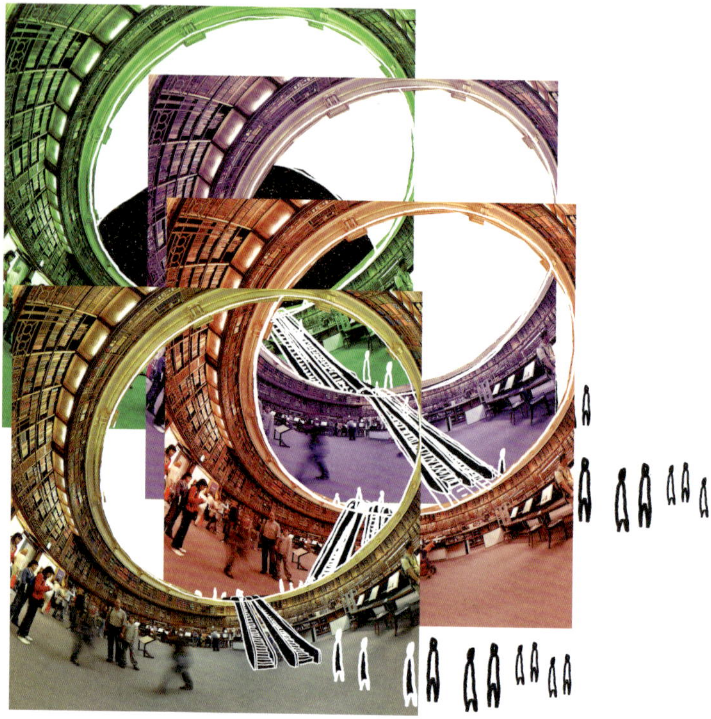

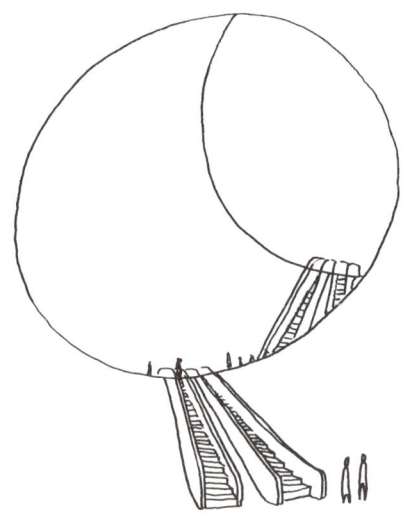

Library of Birmingham
Birmingham, 2008

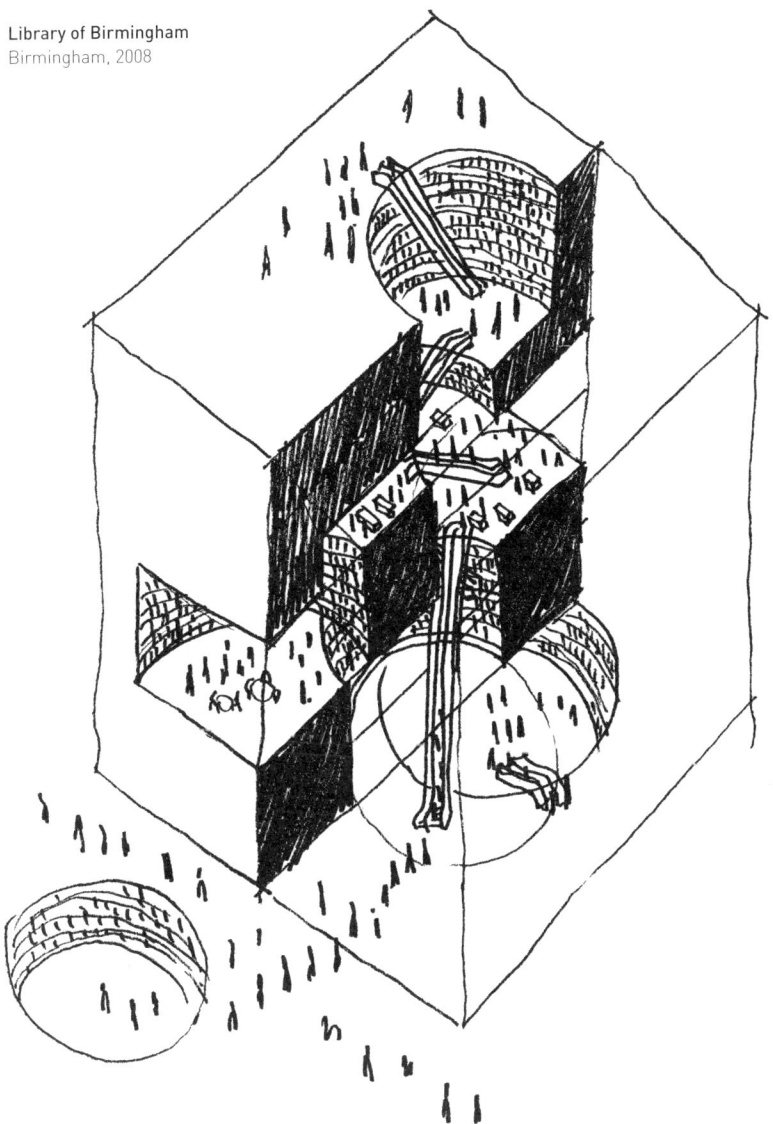

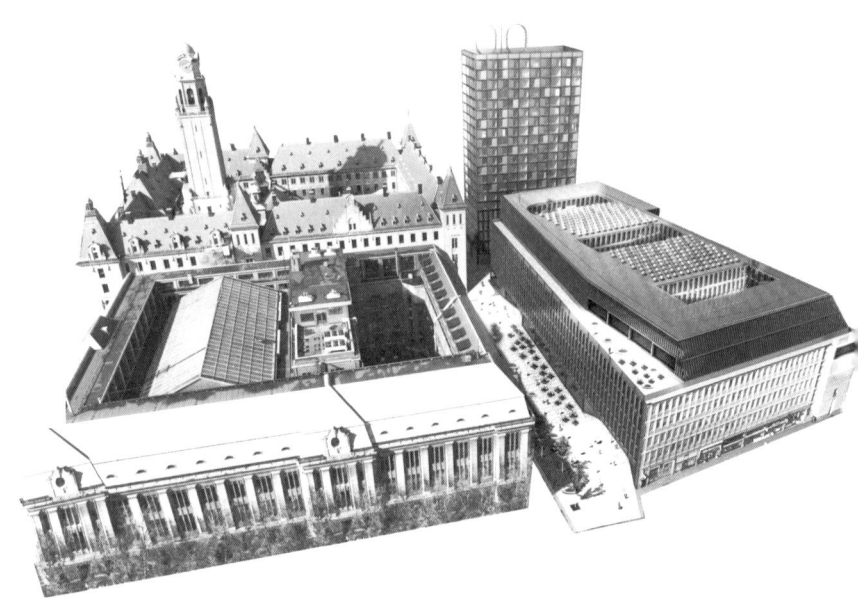

left
City Hall Redevelopment
Rotterdam, 2009

below
Retail Park Square Westermaat
Hengelo, 1999

Modelling

Models, whether rough, sketchy and imperfect, or extremely realistic and detailed, have always been a part of Mecanoo's creative process, ever since its early work. Through models made using a variety of materials, from wood to cardboard, plastic and sheet metal, the practice shapes and handles the work on a small scale, something it could hardly do on paper or even a computer screen. It investigates surfaces, light, voids and solids through the potential offered by the building, or some part of it. The same approach is applied even when the project concerns whole urban lots, a cluster of buildings or even an entire neighborhood or town. The models are made without any aesthetic desire to show the work off in pleasing ways; the technique is recognized as a useful instrument for making direct contact with the architecture before building it on the real scale.

these and following pages
Library Delft University of Technology
Delft, 1993

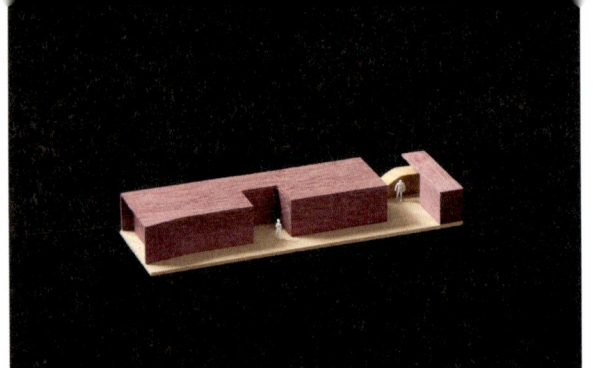

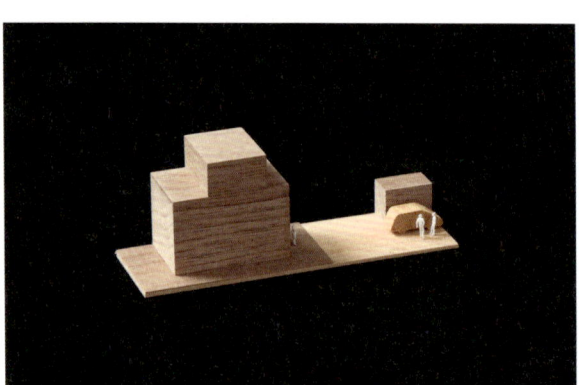

**Waterrijk
residential area**
Eindhoven, 2006

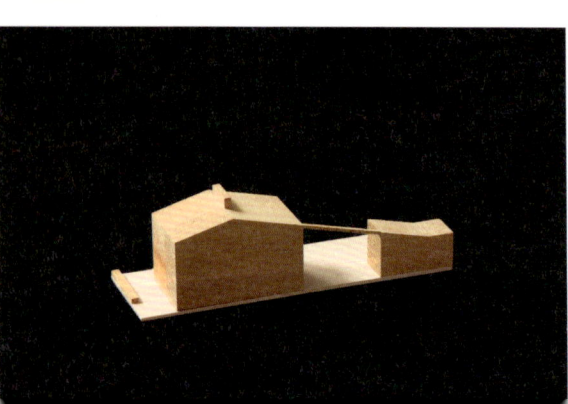

these pages
Castle Ruins Cultural Center
Deurne, 1992

following pages
City Hall Redevelopment
Rotterdam, 2009

left
Montevideo residential tower
Rotterdam, 1999

right
National Historic Museum
Arnhem, 2007

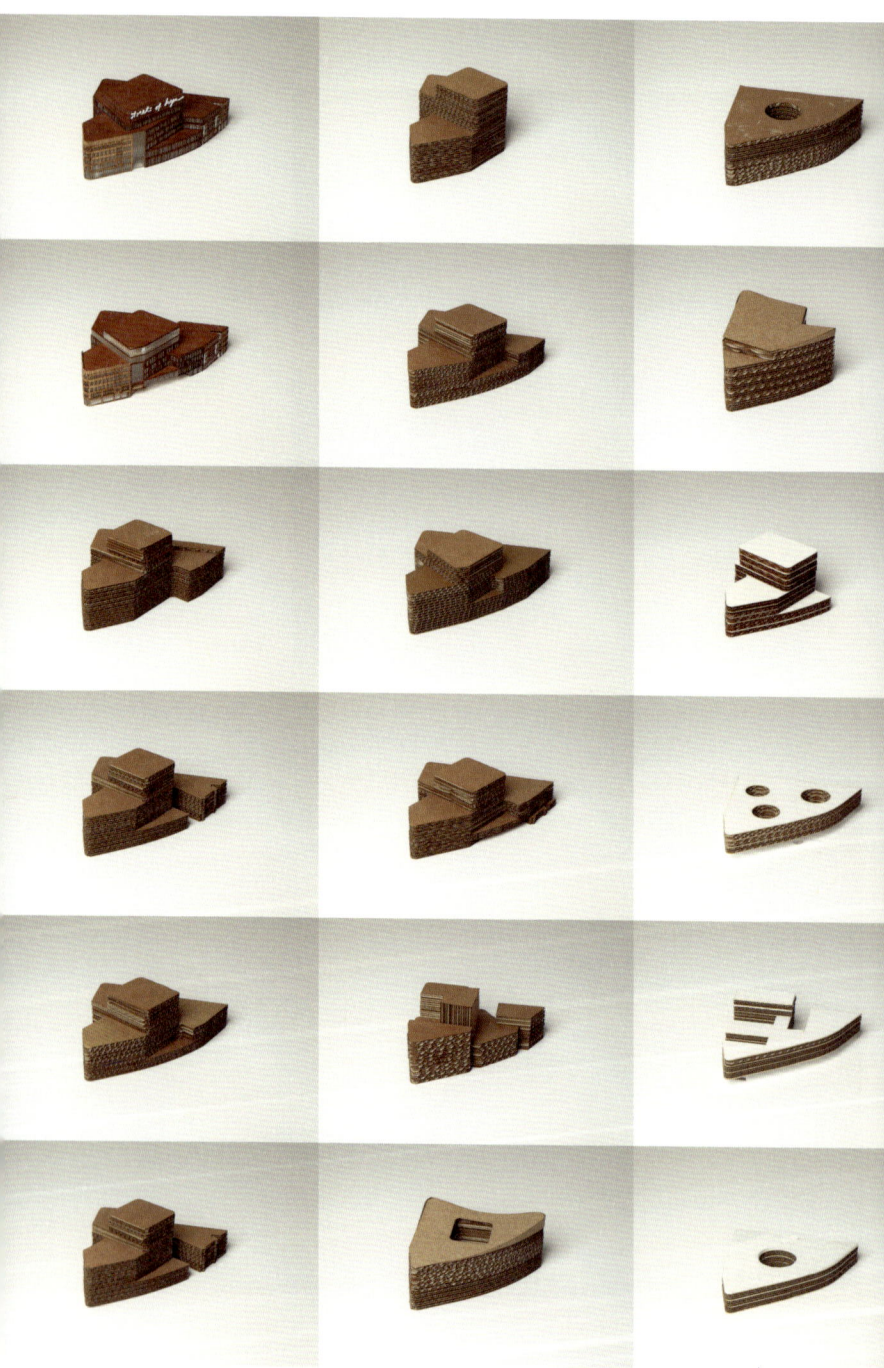

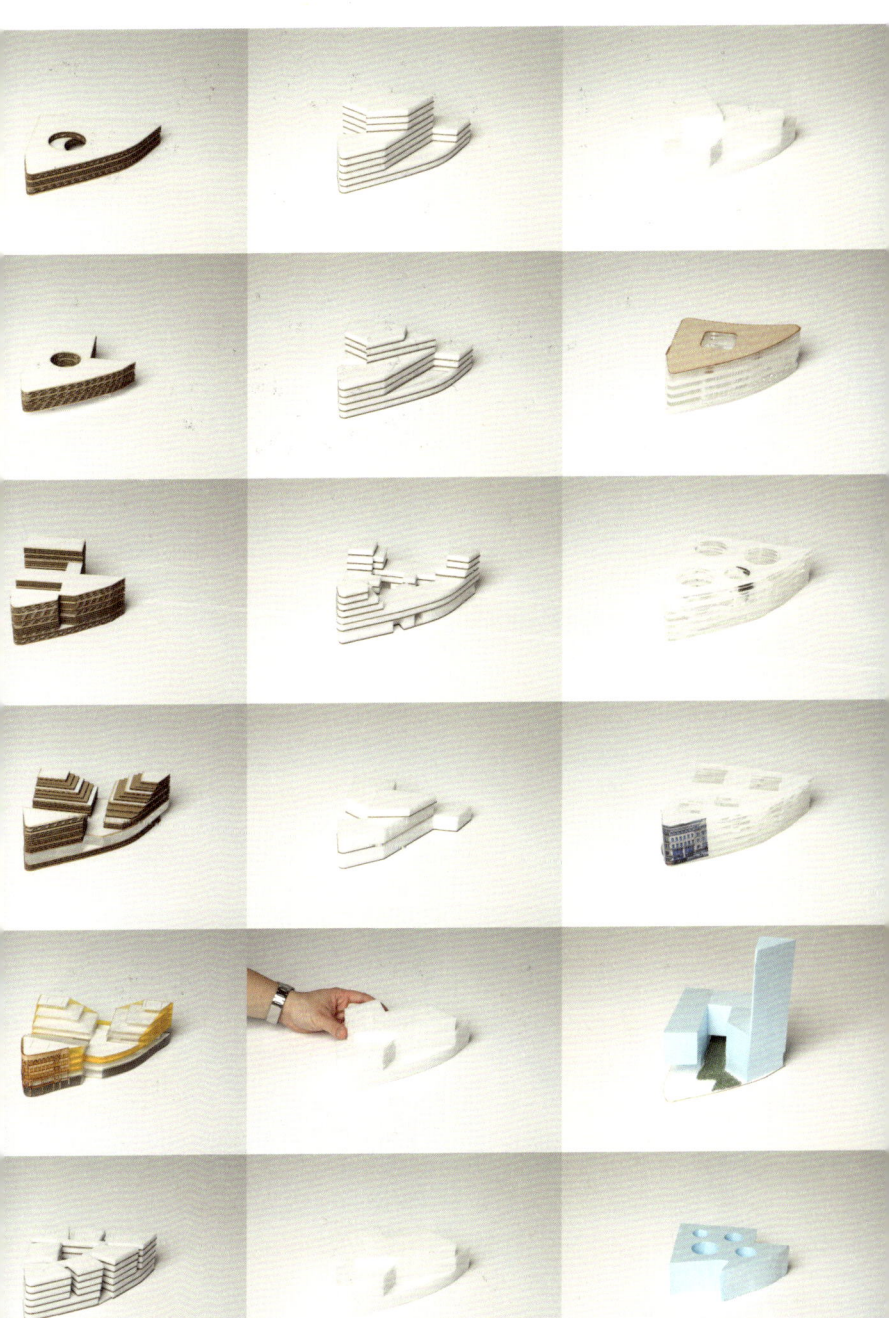

previous pages
Bruce C. Bolling Municipal Building
Boston, 2011

above and right
Montevideo residential tower
Rotterdam, 1999

below
Woonwijk Kanaleneiland masterplan and design
Utrecht, 2000

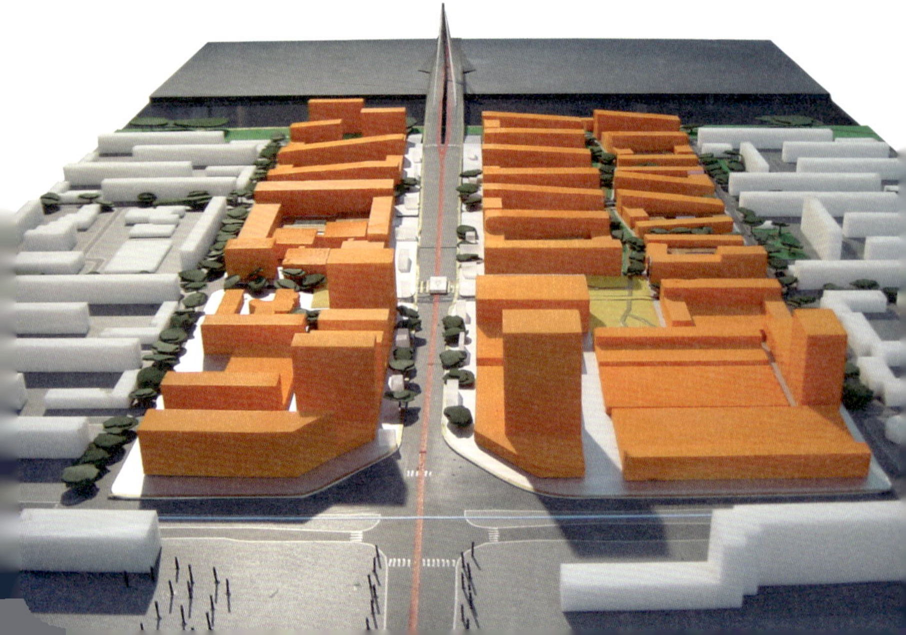

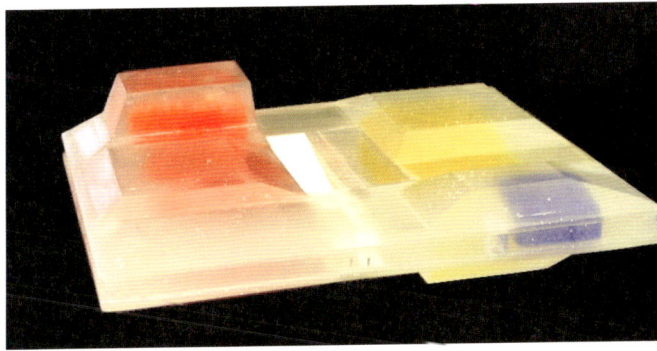

La Llotja Theater and Conference Center
Lleida, 2004

below
Municipal Offices and Train Station
Delft, 2006

right
**Kaap Skil, Maritime
and Beachcombers Museum**
Oudeschild, 2007

Library of Birmingham
Birmingham, 2008

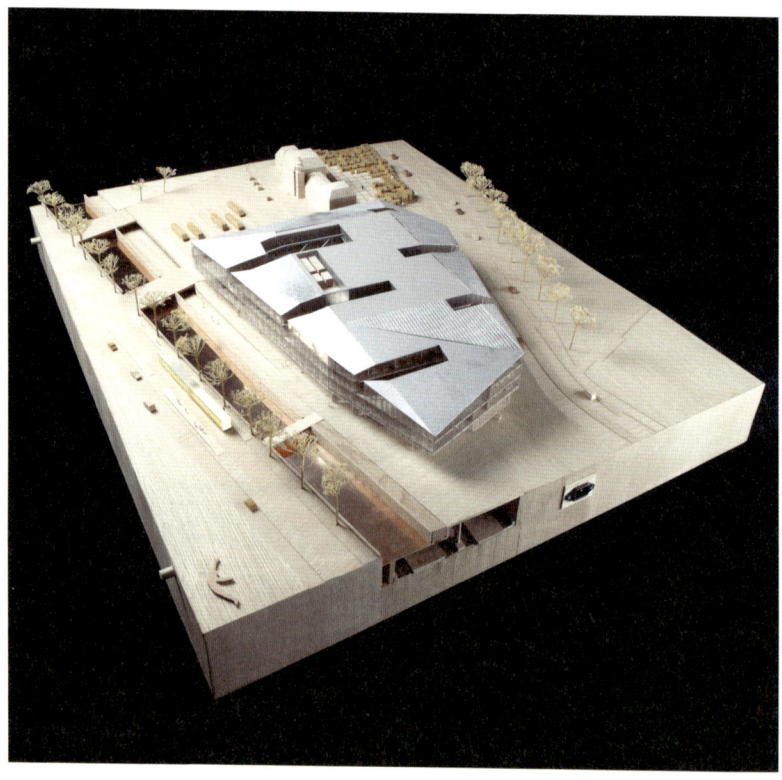

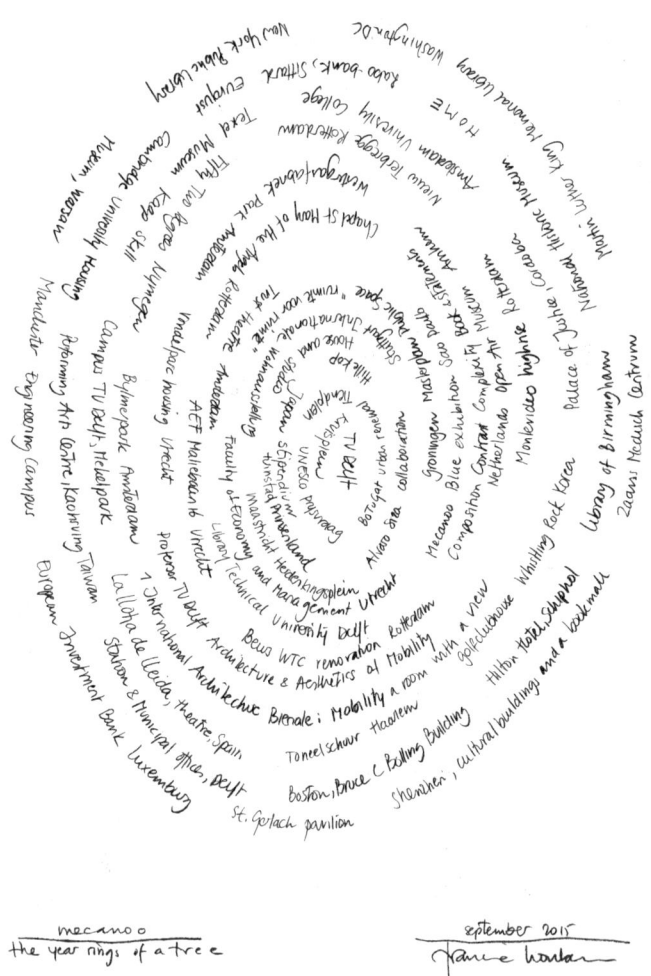

The year rings of a tree
2015
Sketch by Francine Houben

Biography

Officially founded in Delft in 1984, Mecanoo architecten is made up of a creative and multidisciplinary staff that includes architects, interior designers, urban planners, landscape architects, and architectural engineers. The practice is led by Founding Partner and Creative Director Francine Houben, together with Dick van Gameren as Partner/Director Design & Research, Friso van der Steen as Technical Director and Peter Haasbroek as Financial Director.

Extensive experience gained over more than 30 years, together with a clear planning process, allows for Mecanoo's designs to be realized with a high level of technical skill and great attention to detail. Approaching a project with a multidisciplinary team gives every project the opportunity to be explored and developed holistically from the outset; combining social design ideas with cutting edge technology in sustainability and engineering to deliver the most effective architectural response for both the client and user. Mecanoo's work has been widely honored by the architectural community.

Mecanoo - named after the British model construction set invented in 1898 - was born out of an innovative winning design proposal for a competition in 1984 which proposed a flexible social housing project in the center of Rotterdam. Since then the company has continued to grow and diversify, designing projects that range from houses, neighborhoods, skyscrapers, cities, polders and schools to theaters, libraries, hotels, museums and even a chapel.

Discovering unexpected solutions for the specifics of program and context is the foremost challenge in all of Mecanoo's assignments. Each design is considered in terms of its cultural setting, place and time. As such, each project is treated as a unique design statement embedded within its context and orchestrated specifically for the people who use it. Within the practice are knowledge centers which enable Mecanoo to stay current on technological and design innovations in sustainability, eco-engineering, technology, education and learning, high-rise and mobility. Preoccupied not by a focus on form, but on process, consultation, context, urban scale and integrated sustainable design strategies, the practice creates culturally significant buildings with a human touch.

Creative Director Francine Houben holds Honorary Fellowships of the Royal Institute of British Architects (RIBA), the American Institute of Architects (AIA) and the Royal Architectural Institute of Canada (RAIC). She was also granted lifelong membership to the Akademie der Künste in Berlin. Francine Houben was professor of mobility aesthetics at Delft University of Technology and also taught at the universities of Harvard and Yale. As curator of the First International Architecture Biennale Rotterdam, she brought the theme of the aesthetics of mobility to the forefront of international design consciousness. She holds Honorary Doctorates from Utrecht University and Université de Mons. In 2015, Queen Máxima of the Netherlands presented her the prestigious Prins Bernhard Cultuurfonds Prize for her entire oeuvre.

Credits

Francesca Serrazanetti
PhD in Architecture, she lectures and researches at the Architectural Design Department at the Politecnico di Milano. She works as independent curator on exhibitions and publishing projects, writing on architecture, design and theatre. She is editor of the magazine 'Stratagemmi'.

Matteo Schubert
Director of the culture department of ABCittà s.c.r.l. and the architecture firm Alterstudio Partners srl, with which he has carried out numerous cultural and architectural projects for private and public sector clients, winning national and international awards. He has developed and curated various events, exhibitions and publications.

All photography and illustrations copyright by Mecanoo architecten, excluding:

Harry Cock (Page 9, 11, 12, 14, 19, 142-143)
Jenneke ter Horst (Page 23)
Boston Archive (Page 75)
Pieter Vandermeer (Page 119 top and middle, 120, 121)